Simple, Generous, Open

Simple, Generous, Open

Charlotte Gale

CANTERBURY
PRESS
Norwich

© Charlotte Gale 2024

Published in 2024 by Canterbury Press
Editorial office
3rd Floor, Invicta House,
110 Golden Lane,
London EC1Y 0TG, UK

www.canterburypress.co.uk

Canterbury Press is an imprint of Hymns Ancient & Modern Ltd
(a registered charity)

Hymns Ancient & Modern® is a registered trademark of
Hymns Ancient & Modern Ltd
13A Hellesdon Park Road, Norwich,
Norfolk NR6 5DR, UK

Scripture quotations are from New Revised Standard Version Bible:
Anglicized Edition, copyright © 1989, 1995 National Council
of the Churches of Christ in the United States of America.
Used by permission. All rights reserved worldwide.

The Author has asserted her right under the Copyright, Designs and
Patents Act 1988 to be identified as the Author of this Work

British Library Cataloguing in Publication data

A catalogue record for this book is available
from the British Library

ISBN: 978-1-78622-625-9

Typeset by Regent Typesetting
Printed and bound by
CPI Group (UK) Ltd

The Skylight

You were the one for skylights, I opposed
Cutting into the seasoned tongue-and-groove
Of pitch pine. I liked it low and closed,
Its claustrophobic, nest-up-in-the-roof
Effect, I liked the snuff-dry feeling,
The perfect, trunk-lid fit of the old ceiling.
Under there, it was all hutch and hatch,
The blue slates kept the heat like midnight thatch.

But when the slates came off, extravagant
Sky entered and held surprise wide open,
For days I felt like an inhabitant
Of that house where the man sick of the palsy
Was lowered through the roof, had his sins forgiven,
Was healed, took up his bed and walked away.

Seamus Heaney[1]

For the wonderful community of people
that is St Clare's, without whom
there would be no story to tell.

Love God, serve God; everything is in that.
St Clare of Assisi

Contents

Foreword

A few weeks ago I joined the community of St Clare's for their Sunday worship. It was the end of the summer break and people were still returning after holiday, so it was a small gathering that lunchtime. However, the warmth of the welcome was huge. Each person was embraced with love and care, everyone had a place, and all knew that they belonged.

That Sunday they were saying goodbye to a family on the move. For the toddler, this was home and family, for the parents they had found something of their identity growing within this community. Messages of care and prayer were placed in a memory box to be taken and read to encourage them as they took a new vocational path. The community grieved their loss while sharing the joy of new beginnings.

Stories were shared, bread was broken, blessings were spoken. And afterwards, we all joined in eating together and unpacking the new season's stock for the shop. As we uncovered crib figures, children's books and musical instruments, I listened to the stories of how people had found a home here.

This book is a deeply personal telling of the story of how St Clare's came about, the vision that gave birth to this new worshipping community, and the challenges faced along the way. It reflects on vocation and the call of God on our lives. It will move you and cause you to think about the nature of our ecclesiology as the people of God. What might we learn from it as the Church of England, and how might it shape our outreach and growth in the future?

The twelfth-century saint Clare of Assisi was someone influenced by her contemporary, 'the poor little man', St Francis. Both of them came from families of privilege and wealth yet found themselves encountering God in a very personal way, calling them to relinquish the comfort of what they knew. It took Francis on the road with his band of brothers. For Clare, it meant founding a community around principles of simplicity, holiness and prayer.

St Clare's at the Cathedral has also been about stepping away from the comfort of what is known and established, and building a new community. One where all are welcome, where dreams are shared, and hope is renewed. It has drawn those who have felt rootless, rejected or restless.

On the wall above the Eucharistic table in gold script are St Clare's words: *Love God, Serve God; everything is in that.* This is the invitation which characterizes the community here, the desire that all should encounter God for themselves. The values of simplicity, generosity and openness have shaped this community to be the sort of place where any can call in, online, in person, to browse and shop, to gather for worship, and most importantly where they can hear the whisper of God's welcome.

The Rt Revd Ruth Worsley
Acting Bishop of Coventry

Boxes

Jenny: Hello, Naomi and Charlotte! Do you still make outfits for clergy women? (Have I remembered correctly that you did?!) If so, do you ever need clergy shirts to cut up and use the collars? I'm asking because Kevin Mayhew's (a large supplier of all things church) has some that are destined for the skip. Women's and men's, various colours, brand new. Give me a shout asap if you'd like us to send you a bundle? Jenny xx

Naomi: That's so kind; would we be able to simply sell them if that would be acceptable? If not, I'll take as many as are available either way. Thank you for thinking of us.

Jenny: There are ... LOTS available. Do you have colour and size preferences?

Naomi: Do you think they'd allow us to sell them?

Charlotte: We'll take all they've got and then see if we can sell them. If not, we could still distribute through the shop for postage which would be good marketing.

Jenny: Just women's, or men's as well?

Naomi: Both. We are always getting asked for men's!

Jenny: When I say lots, there are like 48 boxes. How many do you think you can handle? KM's say you can sell if you pay postage. Or you could come and see us and collect them!

Charlotte: Wow, this is amazing. Where are they now?

Naomi: Of course we should pay postage if we are selling them. Could you give me an idea of how many in a box? Just trying to think about storage.

Jenny: This is an example of box contents, they are all quite random. They are currently in a warehouse here at KM, which needs clearing.

Picture of an enormous cardboard box, with a handwritten list of contents, which totals 25 clerical shirts in a range of sizes and colours.

Charlotte: There's an enormous cathedral next door. Surely we can find somewhere ...

Naomi: I think we should just say we will take them all.

Charlotte: We'll def take them all.

And so it was, that the week before Christmas 2022 I took delivery of 48 enormous boxes crammed full of unsold clergy shirts, still in their original packaging. I started by stowing as many as I could in the tiny kitchen at the back of St Clare's – a church and gift shop based at Coventry Cathedral. I squeezed a couple of them in the tiny storeroom, which was, as usual, already overflowing with second-hand books. Then I created a wall of boxes, three high, along the back of the worship space, and tried to make it look festive by covering it in a green cloth and putting the large angel and shepherds from the nativity set on the top of them.

Naomi, my partner, was having none of this, so then I carried them over to St Michael's house, adjacent to the cathedral, and piled them in the committee room, figuring that there wouldn't be many meetings in there this close to Christmas, and I wasn't going to have time to do anything with them until the new year anyway, not least as this was always the busiest week of the year at St Clare's.

On our first Sunday back in January, after the service, members of the community went and collected the boxes, and we began the process of opening and sorting them all. Only then did we realize quite what a treasure trove it was. An extraordinary gift that would hopefully ensure the financial viability for another year of St Clare's, a ministry I had poured my heart and soul into for the last five years.

This is a book about St Clare's at the Cathedral. In a time when the Church of England has an ambitious target to establish 10,000 new worshipping communities by 2030, we increasingly felt that we had a story to tell about our community, launched in 2017, that might encourage and even inspire others. We have so far kept going through a global pandemic, a period of intense financial uncertainty in the wider economy, and significant changes in the diocese that at times seemed to threaten our future.

It is also a book about me. It turns out that in order to write the story of St Clare's, I had to tell quite a lot of my own story, discovering in the process how much God uses all that we are, and all that we have ever done, in each subsequent chapter of our lives. It is also a book about Naomi. The Revd Naomi Nixon (at time of writing the CEO of the Student Christian Movement) has been my partner in life, really since we met on the first day of theological college in 1997, and we have also lived and ministered together since 2004.

St Clare's is unusual compared to many of the new worshipping communities that we see springing up around us, both locally and nationally. It is firmly rooted in the central and eucharistic tradition of the Church of England. But we are also rooted in the word, faithfully grappling with Scripture and thinking about what it says to us in our increasingly complex world. It is co-led by me and Naomi, two priests who already had considerable experience and had been ordained a long time when we set up St Clare's; we haven't yet stumbled across any other mid-ministry pioneers. And it's progressive. We are an unashamedly rainbow community, embracing diversity of sexuality, gender, race, age and more. We are blessed with members who are neurodiverse, others who are differently abled and many of us at one time or another have had mental health struggles. On the face of it we are a pretty motley crew, but together we are transformed by the Spirit into the beautiful body of Christ. Our worship space is also our retail space, selling gifts, books, church supplies and worship resources both locally and nationally through our online store.

There are lots of books about the theory and theology of fresh expressions, pioneer churches, new worshipping communities ... whatever you want to call them. But I've never been much good at reading them. What I do love to read is a story.

This is ours.

How We Got Here

Trust in the L*ORD*, *and do good;*
  so you will live in the land, and enjoy security.
Take delight in the L*ORD*,
  and he will give you the desires of your heart.
Commit your way to the L*ORD*;
  trust in him, and he will act.
(Psalm 37.3–5)

The Third Sunday of Lent

Pick a Sunday, any Sunday… this is just one.

Naomi and I arrive at St Clare's at just before 11.30 a.m. Having spent nearly a decade doing 8 a.m. services every Sunday, the decadence of leaving the house at 11.15 a.m. still delights me. Today I'm feeling especially pleased with myself as I managed to make us cheese and piccalilli sandwiches before leaving, so we didn't have to stop at Greggs on the way to pick up vegan rolls, which has become a bit of a habit of late.

Evan, our churchwarden, is already here, and he and Gavin, who is very new and keen and usually waiting when we arrive, have already started setting up for church. We're greeted by the smell of freshly brewing coffee, and the kettle is on for tea. By the time people start arriving, there will be coffee, decaf coffee, a range of teabags, hot chocolate sachets and hot water ready, along with milk and oat milk. Snacks include crisps, biscuits and fruit.

As Evan and Gavin set up the refreshments, Naomi sets up communion. Nothing complicated, just a corporal with a chalice and paten on it. She fills the chalice with wine and puts a bread roll in the paten, covering it with a purificator. The bread is lactose and gluten free so all can share in the one bread. Once she's done that, she hangs a purple stole over the front of the communion table. We don't robe, but whichever of us is presiding at communion puts on a stole at the preparation of the table.

Gavin has started putting out the service sheets on the chairs. We use the same printed liturgy each week, along with an A5 sheet with the Bible reading on one side and the hymn words on the other. He is stepping gingerly as the floor of the worship space is covered in a thin layer of sand. The worship space is round. The communion table is at one side, part of a circle with 16 chairs in the front row, and a further eight chairs in the second row. There is also a stack of folding chairs in case we need them. In one corner, but still in the circle, there is a rug and lots of children's toys.

There isn't usually sand on the floor. There is usually a second rug. But during Lent, we are using sand each week in our service, as we work our way through the Old Testament readings in the lectionary, which this year follows the story of God's covenant with his people.

On the first Sunday of Lent the sand was piled up in front of the communion table, representing Mount Ararat. A toy Noah's Ark was perched on top, with all the animals heading off down the mountain.

On the second Sunday of Lent, the sand was a bit more spread out, to represent the lands where Abraham and Sarah travelled after being called into a covenant with God. It was piled up against a large picture of numerous stars in the sky. On the sand we put two dolls to be Abraham and Sarah. We make sure that all the dolls we sell in the shop come in a range of skin tones, so it was no problem to pick two that looked Middle Eastern, even if their clothing was very twenty-first century!

This week the sand is spread out to fill the whole worship space so no one can avoid walking on it. As we set up for church it is already looking quite trodden on.

Finally, Evan sets up the laptop in the centre of the space, for those joining us via Zoom. We are ready.

As people arrive, they all comment on the sand. Some people

confidently walk across it, others sneak into the back row of chairs to avoid it. Most people get a drink before sitting down. By midday, when the service starts, most of the chairs are full and there is a buzz of chatter.

Just after noon, I pick up our singing bowl and start to make it hum. It's taken me a while to get the hang of it, but once you've got the knack, it makes a beautiful continuous bell-like hum, which gradually increases in volume. As people become aware of it, the conversations begin to still. Once I have everyone's attention, I greet them.

'The Lord be with you.'

They respond: 'And also with you.'

Then come the notices, which include a welcome and brief explanation of how the service works for any newcomers. I keep talking longer than I might as more people arrive. Everyone who comes in exclaims about the sand and we all laugh. By the time I have finished the notices most of the chairs are full.

The service itself lasts just under an hour. It is a simple communion service using the bare bones of Common Worship. Music is played from my phone through a Bluetooth speaker. We always start with a piece of music and have a hymn at communion; sometimes there is more music, maybe during the intercessions or as a meditation.

The Bible reading – usually just one – is read by Amy. There is no rota or planning, someone just offers when we get there.

I then give a homily. I don't move or stand up, but just stay in my seat. A couple of times, people chip in or ask questions. When I've finished I invite people to share their thoughts on what I've said. Two or three people do that. Today, Tom's contribution is very academic, while Julia's is totally from the heart, responding to what God is saying to her.

I've explained that the sand this week represents the desert where the people walked for 40 years, as they learned afresh to be the people of God after leaving Egypt. I then invite people to consciously walk on the sand, thinking about their own walk with God. I play a piece of music as we do this, a version of some of Psalm 119. People are careful and respectful as they walk, only three or four people stand at a time. Towards the end, one-year-old Mia, who has only been walking for a few weeks, toddles across the sand with a big smile on her face. We all share in her simple joy.

When the music ends I lead us into intercessions. This week they are spoken prayers, based on each of the Ten Commandments. Before we get to the Peace, I feel it's right to ask how people felt about walking on the sand. This was the right thing to do, as there are a couple more really heartfelt contributions.

As we are about to share the Peace, another person arrives: Annie, who has had her eighteenth birthday this week. We all congratulate her and spontaneously sing Happy Birthday before sharing the Peace. Before the Covid-19 pandemic we used to all stand and hug one another, but now we stay seated and wave and speak to one another and to the people on the Zoom screen.

While this happens, I stand and move behind the communion table and put on my purple stole, ready to preside.

Everyone else remains seated during the Eucharistic Prayer. We vary which prayer we use, but the service sheet only has the responses on, which means that people tend to look at me (or Naomi) rather than down at words, which I love. Sometimes we sing the Sanctus, today we don't.

After the Lord's Prayer and the breaking of bread, everyone stands to receive. Before I set off round the circle, I press play on my phone, and the hymn starts. People sing as they receive. I move round the circle with the bread. I love the act of placing the consecrated bread in people's hands. It has always been a really special thing for me. I love the way that as you get to know people, their hands tell their stories. Hands that have tended children and caressed lovers. Hands that have worked hard, hands that have fought off abusers, hands that have held loved ones as they died. It is in giving communion that I most feel the love that comes from having 'the cure of souls'.

The wine is passed around from person to person and arrives back at the communion table not long after me. Everyone is now singing loudly.

Once the hymn finishes, there is the post-communion prayer and the blessing, and the service ends. But no one rushes off.

Some people go and get another drink. Some people move to chat to someone in a different place, others simply get their sandwiches (or impressive-looking salads) out and start eating. Others nip out to the shops to get something.

As I'm chatting to one of our students, I notice that Annie's mum has taken an enormous chocolate cake out of a box and is surreptitiously putting candles on it. I pick up the matches from the cabinet next to the communion table and take them over to her. We of course have to sing Happy Birthday again, as Annie blows out the candles. We congratulate her on making it to church, if a bit late, as her mum tells us that she'd been out very late the night before.

Gradually after half an hour or so, people start to leave. We also get the odd shopper coming in, and I sell some rosary beads. Shoppers often come in when we are worshipping, as, however hard we try, almost no one reads the sign saying we are closed for church. But it's OK, if they don't realize then someone, often Evan, goes and explains.

It's also Evan who usually does the washing-up.

Today, we are finally cleared up and ready to leave at about 2.30 p.m. Sometimes it's earlier, sometimes later. Sometimes we do 'shop jobs' and invite people to stay on to help with a new window display or with packaging and sorting stock.

But not today. On the way home in the car we chat about the service. We always seem to end up commenting on how amazing this community is, and how incredibly blessed we are to lead it. We arrive home spiritually fed and emotionally uplifted. We give thanks.

Itchy feet

Once every six weeks, while I was Vicar of Lillington in Leamington Spa (the role I had before starting St Clare's), I would visit my spiritual director in the lovely village of Southam (it's of no relevance to this story, but it's where Justin Welby was once the vicar) at an old convent, now a retreat house. There I would spend an hour chatting to the wonderful Val, an elderly

Roman Catholic laywoman, whose gentle wisdom supported a good number of the Anglican clergy in the diocese. After the chat, she would disappear, and usually you would have the whole house to yourself for a few hours, to think, to read, to pray, until she would return for a second chat about what insights you had gained.

I had been in my post for about seven years and I was getting itchy feet. I loved the place and the people, but there were the beginnings of a quiet restlessness in me, that sense that maybe God was calling me on to something new.

The trouble was, I had no idea what.

I did, however, have very firm ideas about what I did not want to do.

I didn't feel that I could face starting again in a third incumbency, not least as I didn't think I could find anywhere better than the wonderful place I was. Various people, in the way that they do, thought that surely I would make an excellent archdeacon, but it's a job entirely unsuited to my skill set and while I may be *able* to do it (and that's a pretty conditional may), it would probably make me deeply miserable. I toyed with the idea of cathedral ministry and gave serious consideration to applying for the Canon Pastor job at Coventry Cathedral, but when I read the profile, nothing in it called to me. There was a time when I had thought I would love to be a diocesan director of ordinands (DDO), but having spent a few years as one of the team of associate DDOs in the diocese, I had fulfilled that calling as far as it felt right to. I was stuck. Every job I considered just didn't appeal.

And so I decided that maybe God wanted me to stay where I was, as I couldn't see any other doors opening. That was where I had got to that morning in Southam, and my plan was to try and envision what I would be working towards if I stayed where I was for another seven years. What was my vision for the church?

I thought of the people that we weren't reaching. We had almost no one between the ages of 18 and 30. We did lots of weddings and baptisms, and young couples would enthusiastically come to church in the run-up to the service, and quite a few would carry on coming for a while afterwards, but most of them gradually drifted away. It was a great church, but some people were falling through the cracks. Why was that?

It was partly, I suspected, because of the make-up of the current church. The majority of our members were over 60. There were also younger folks, and we had a Sunday club and a youth group, but when you walked in, the impression you got was older, not least as they were the ones who attended most regularly and, having more time, took on more of the upfront visible roles. Then there was the style of worship. If you like organ music, that's great, and ours was excellent, but it's not for everyone. The building itself was also a hindrance. There were only a few pews where you could see past the chunky pillars, and these were usually filled by prompt regulars.

I tried to envisage a church with a variety of styles of music, maybe with a circle of chairs rather than rows of pews. I wondered whether we needed to start a new thing aimed at younger people, as the church was pretty full on a Sunday morning.

But that brought me to the next problem. My capacity. I was already vicar of two parishes, usually did three services on a Sunday, was area dean and a member of General Synod. If I was going to do something new, then something would have to go.

But most of all, I was concerned that the radical change needed to bring in those missing people would destroy the very character of the church that I loved. A church that was thriving, and that really worked for a lot of people. I wasn't sure if it was possible for one church to work for everyone.

I wrote all this down in my prayer journal and offered it to God. I also told Val, who assured me she would also be praying about it. God must surely have some ideas about what next; I just needed them to be communicated to me.

Skylights

Naomi was at our cottage in the valleys of South Wales, doing research, and a couple of days later I drove down to join her with Dolly, our miniature Schnauzer. This meant we had two cars there, which was unusual. The cottage was built in the mid-nineteenth century, with thick stone walls, bound together with mortar gleaming with black coal dust. It had originally been a straightforward two up, two down, but at some point a tiny kitchen and bathroom extension had been added to the back, and the two downstairs rooms knocked through into one. What makes it different from the countless other such cottages is its height. It's semi-detached, and the story goes that two brothers built the cottages, and they were unusually tall for the time, so built their homes with higher ceilings, and a steeply pitched roof. The loft was one huge open space across both houses when we bought it, and a requirement of the mortgage was that we had a fire wall built to divide it into two. So we discovered this high, dark, cavernous space, full of ancient Christmas decorations and a couple of skeletons of long-dead rats. My uncle, a builder, came and built the wall for us, and assured us that there was no sign of any live rats.

But at some point, the rats returned. Lying in bed at night you would hear them running around above you, sounding for all the world like they were the size of wolfhounds. It did not make for a peaceful night's sleep. They chewed through the electrics, so we had to have the whole cottage rewired, and after that we began a concerted campaign to wipe them out. But however much we poisoned them, trapped them or tried to put them off with devices emitting unpleasant noises, they kept coming back. This dark, quiet space, in a mostly unoccupied house, was just too enticing.

After much reading on the matter, we were convinced that what was needed was light. We came up with a plan. We would clear the loft of all the rubbish and ancient insulation, get the floors boarded and put in a skylight. Hopefully this would finally persuade the rats to leave. I should say at this point that it was really Naomi's plan. She has extraordinary vision to see what needs to be done, and the drive to do it. To me, it seemed like a lot of work and a lot of money, and I wasn't sure I was up to it. Left on my own, I would probably have just gone to bed with earplugs, never opened the loft hatch, and tried to pretend we weren't sharing our cottage with these furry creatures.

But by now, I had known Naomi long enough to trust her ideas and her ability to get things done, and so we set about finding a builder. We found Anthony, a carpenter who had just set up his own business, having previously worked for large construction firms. He came and looked at the situation, and pointed out that if we were boarding the floor and adding a skylight, surely we might as well also insulate and plaster the walls and make a room. It wouldn't cost that much more. And if we were doing that, it wouldn't be that much more to add a staircase so you could access this new room. It would mean moving the boiler, but that would be manageable. And if you're doing all that, you'll want at least two skylights. He also tried to persuade us to put in a dormer and a kitchenette, but we drew the line after the second skylight.

And so we spent every penny of our savings, and a bit more, and endured six months of chaos and plaster dust, and a builder on the edge of a nervous breakdown (running his own business was proving much trickier than anticipated) and who required every ounce of our combined pastoral skills to keep going, until finally we had a room. It was large and light, with an exposed stone wall at one end, and a beautifully crafted staircase at the other, which Anthony had poured all his love into, carpentry being what he really wanted to be doing. Naomi put her interior design skills to work, and we waxed the wooden floor and staircase, papered the walls and hunted for furniture and fittings. Finally, it was finished. It is the most beautiful room. Accessed by a door in the back bedroom, up a secret staircase, it is both light and spacious, but also cosy and private. We love this room. Possibly the most expensive solution to a rat problem ever, but so worth it.

I can't remember how long we were in Wales for after I joined Naomi, probably just a couple of days, but late in the afternoon, on the day we were heading home, we went up to the loft room with a cup of tea and talked again about the future. We had talked about it a lot. I told her about my quiet morning. We went through every type of job we could think of in the Church of England, trying to find one that fitted, but nothing called to me. I was at a point in my ministry when lots of well-meaning people were expecting me to be ambitious, and kept suggesting various important (and to me immensely boring) sounding jobs I should consider. I had no interest in any of them.

Eventually, Naomi spoke the words that would change our lives.

'I think we need to start a new church.'

Apparently, I was silent. Unlike with every other suggestion, there was no quick retort or immediate reason why it was wrong. But then my brain engaged, and I was both horrified and dismissive. That seemed just too hard, too impossible, and so risky. But somehow, we couldn't just pass this idea over like we had all the others. We kept talking and began to think about what it might look like and whether we could really do it. I started worrying about the idea failing before we had even begun to imagine what such a church might be. But although on the face of it it seemed a mad idea for two priests in very conventional Church of England jobs, between us we had a surprising amount of pioneering experience. Just four months after I was ordained, the church where I was curate planted a church on a large new housing estate on the edge of the parish. My training incumbent was keen that once I was priested, I should take responsibility for this new worshipping community, setting the vision and pattern for their future. I was initially sceptical; it seemed too much and way beyond me as a new priest. But Naomi reminded me that in my previous job, I was part of a team that had transformed the composting industry in the UK, and that I had set up and run the Composting Association, a trade body with over 300 members when I set off for theological college. And so with her encouragement I had said yes to the challenge, and had a wonderful two and a half years leading the Warwick Gates Community Church, which is now Heathcote Parish Church, a grown-up church with its own vicar and a thriving ministry. Naomi, meanwhile, having completed her curacy in Hereford Diocese and moved in with me, was working as a Further Education chaplain at a large college. Everything she did was pioneering, from carving out a tiny office from a storage cupboard, to setting up and running a youthwork course (concurrently training to be a teacher), the income from which would fund the fledgling chaplaincy.

We talked about what our vision might be for a new church, where we might want it, and who it would be for. It soon became a really fun conversation, as we imagined this future church. But it didn't feel real. It was just a fantasy. I don't think I had any idea at that moment that we might really do it. It was like when we had first talked about the loft room. Naomi had a vision of skylights, when I was just trying to manage in the dark.

We talked for so long that by the time we packed up and left, it was not only much later than we had intended leaving but very dark and very stormy. We set off in our two cars, hoping to be home by 10.30 p.m. Things did not go to plan. The weather was awful. There was driving rain, and the visibility was terrible. At the time, the Heads of the Valley Road, our route out of Wales, was undergoing a massive facelift and the road was regularly closed overnight. By the time I reached the major roadworks, it was gone 8 p.m., the road had been closed for the night and a diversion was in place. The diversion was a challenge, even in daylight and sunshine. It was long and winding, and very up and down. At night, in the pouring rain, it was horrendous, exhausting and hugely time consuming. It was before the era of reliable Satnavs, so there was nothing to do but try and follow the infrequent yellow diversion signs. I felt as if I was crawling along, trying to avoid endless cones and other cars. At least once I had to retrace my route, having gone the wrong way, and went round most roundabouts several times as I desperately tried to work out which way I was supposed to be going. The driving rain was incessant.

As I drove, concentrating hard on the dark wet road, my mind was turning over and over the conversation we had had. Was this just a fantasy? Could this really be something we could do? Could this be my calling? Was it even possible? I offered the whole thing to God and kept driving, by now exhausted and immensely grateful finally to get to the end of the diversion.

I needed a break. I spotted with relief the new Starbucks that had recently been built seemingly just for us, halfway between our two homes. I pulled in and went to get a coffee. A few minutes later, who should walk in the door but Naomi, having had the same idea. We laughed, and sat down, and started chatting about the terrible journey so far. And then it became clear that, as we had been driving, the Holy Spirit had been at work in both of us. What had seemed like an impossible, crazy idea when we left the cottage had settled into a profound sense of calling. We had no idea how, but somehow, by God's grace, we were going to start a new church.

Time passed and I returned to see Val for another quiet morning.

I had with me a copy of *Accidental Saints* by Nadia Bolz-Weber.[2] I had my usual chat with Val, then when she disappeared I settled down to read. I can't remember if I knew what the book was about before I started.

What I do remember is that it made me cry. I read the first chapter and found myself unexpectedly and unaccountably in tears. I mopped myself up, made a cup of tea and read chapter two. Same thing happened. I read the whole book, pausing to cry after each chapter.

The tears were not because I was sad; I was simply overwhelmed with emotion, and the tears were my body's response. In her book, Nadia tells the story of planting a new church. My response to it confirmed for me that this really was my calling. I wanted to have my own story to tell of starting a new church. A church where all were welcome, especially those who found fitting in just that bit challenging.

---

2 Nadia Bolz-Weber, *Accidental Saints: Finding God in All the Wrong People*, London: Canterbury Press, 2015.

Morris

As things progressed, I had a short-lived attempt at keeping a diary ...

13 March 2016

So I've just sent an email to the Archdeacon. It basically says that we want to take on a wreck of a church in Coventry city centre (abandoned by the church decades ago, and slowly left to deteriorate, it now serves as a somewhat leaky warehouse for a local charity) and start a brand-new church community from nothing. There are no people and no resources – just one seriously dilapidated but nevertheless Grade II listed nineteenth-century Gothic Revival church building.

I'm not quite sure what would possess me to consider such a move. It's not normally the sort of thing I do. I'm willing to step out in faith for God, but this is more like jumping off a cliff. I am very happy in my current ministry; vicar to two healthy, flourishing, well-run and beautifully maintained churches, and Area Dean in the wonderful Warwick and Leamington Deanery. I firmly believe that Royal Leamington Spa is quite possibly the best place to live in the whole world, and mostly I think I could happily stay here for the rest of my life.

But the truth is, after eight years here, I'm feeling restless. I've just had my forty-fifth birthday and don't feel that I've yet reached the job that will ultimately define me. But when I try to think ahead, all the obvious possibilities fill me with a low-level feeling of gloom. I am flattered that other people think I could be an archdeacon, but it sounds an appalling idea to me. There are a couple of big, prestigious churches in the diocese which are both in dire need of a competent, experienced pair of hands and I think that either job could be mine if I wanted it. The trouble is, I don't want it.

Which brings me back to my crazy email. The idea was not completely out of nowhere. We knew about St Mark's (the dilapidated church) because HTB (that's Holy Trinity,

Brompton, who have been planting new churches all over the country) had been to look round and Naomi had joined them as part of her job. They want to set up a resourcing church plant in Coventry and ideally need an empty church to start in; much easier without an existing congregation to persuade. St Mark's is right next door to the rapidly expanding and increasingly well regarded Coventry University. There is no obvious 'student church'. They thought it could be just the place for them. But after looking around they decided against it.

But the building is still there. Right in the heart of student land. Could there still be some scope for this idea, even without all the money and prestige and experience that HTB bring? What if – crazy as it seems – God wants us to take it on?

14 March 2016
The Archdeacon phoned. To be fair, he had a number of things he needed to talk to me about, but nevertheless I let the answerphone speak to him. He mostly talked about the other stuff, but at the end of the message mentioned my crazy email. He wants to talk to me.

The Archdeacon phoned again. The man is persistent. This time I answered. He doesn't think my idea is completely crazy. I backtracked at this point, suddenly anxious that he might take me too seriously. We talked a bit more and I could begin to sense him getting excited. This is a worry. When the Archdeacon gets an idea in his head, there is no stopping him. I think I may have 'unleashed the Morris'.

27 April 2016
In 33 minutes' time the Archdeacon is arriving to discuss our crazy idea. Trouble is, that six weeks on from sending the email, I am beginning to think that it is just crazy, and surely there are other things I could be thinking of doing. A church in this deanery (another St Mark's, in fact), has just failed to appoint a new vicar. They are a large evangelical church but find themselves with two people in same-sex marriages on the PCC (not married to each other!) and are thinking that

*maybe God is calling them to be an inclusive church. I get
excited talking to them. Could it be that God is calling me just
down the road, to a church which could potentially fulfil all
of my desires for the other St Mark's but with a building that
keeps the rain out? I have 28 minutes to somehow rekindle
my excitement and belief in the crazy idea. Maybe I should
pray ...*

*So he's been. I didn't sell the idea terribly well (my initial
email was far more persuasive) but even so, he's basically in
favour of the idea. I feel strangely uncertain now – perhaps
it's a little bit real. We figured a good next step would be for
me to actually see the inside of the building. That's easier said
than done, so I have to email him formally requesting a visit.*

*Naomi is very excited. I worry a bit that it is her vision
more than mine. Can we really do this? I just don't know.*

A working lunch

We went and looked around St Mark's. It was both hugely
exciting but also made me hugely anxious. On reflection, I
think the excitement was because it was a step forward in our
calling, but the anxiety was because it wasn't the right place for
us. We sent a proposal to the Bishop outlining our idea. However, it turned out that in the last few days, HTB had come back
with a new proposal for St Mark's, which the Bishop accepted.
I had a massive sense of relief.

We had pushed on a door, and it had been closed, so maybe
this wasn't what God wanted us to do after all. I tried to put it
to the back of my mind and focus on my current ministry.

But I couldn't do it. As the months passed, it was clear that
the calling was still there, and Naomi certainly wasn't going to
let us just ignore it. We needed a new plan. We talked more and
began to get more of a sense of what this new church was about
and the beginnings of a clearer vision. It was time to get back
in touch with Morris.

Morris took us out to lunch. He was determined that we would
not leave the restaurant until we had cracked the problem of

where this new church would be. I was sceptical but wasn't going to argue with a free lunch at the lovely Saxon Mill. Morris began by trying to persuade us to think about starting the church in Leamington Spa, a town we all knew well. I was currently a vicar at the north end of this lovely Spa town, and Morris had been a vicar at the south end. He had formerly been Area Dean, and I was the current one. It was a town full of students and possibilities, and we knew every inch of it, every empty shop, every church hall, every church! Maybe this was where we needed to focus our search.

But we were determined. However much we loved Leamington, we were sure that the calling was to Coventry, a city often maligned by its own residents and by the wider country, as a metaphorical place you are sent to when shunned. A place scarred by war, and later by deep recession. A place that most of the good folks of Leamington avoided going to, but which had stolen both our hearts. We had always loved Coventry, maybe a bit because it was so maligned. We're always ones to root for the underdog. We had lived there for three years during my first incumbency and Naomi now worked there, as Ministerial Development Advisor for the diocese. We longed to return to live. We knew in our hearts that this was where our new church would be.

And so we started throwing ideas around: an extraordinary brainstorming session, as we tried to think of every possible place a new church could be planted. None of them was right. Every idea one of us came up with was shot down by someone else. Too big, too small, too far out, too expensive, too theologically complicated (taking over a declining Society church[3]). There was a long pause. Maybe my scepticism that we'd crack this today was right.

But then Morris almost jumped out of his seat as he proclaimed:

'I've got it!'

---

3 The Society (or, more fully, The Society under the patronage of Saint Wilfrid and Saint Hilda) is an ecclesial body of parishes who have sought alternative episcopal oversight, as they do not recognize the ordination of women as priests or bishops.

We looked at him, not imagining for a minute that he really had got it, but cocked our heads politely, waiting to hear this great revelation. It was not what we were expecting.

'The cathedral gift shop! That's where your new church should be.'

The story goes that when the great Basil Spence designed the extraordinary and wonderful building that is Coventry Cathedral, he was so focused on the great and grand vision that he didn't pay a lot of attention to practicalities. Power points, toilets and decent acoustics were in short supply. It also didn't occur to him to think about the commercial aspects of tourism, so there was nowhere to put a shop, or any kind of visitor centre. With countless thousands of people expected to come to see the completed cathedral, something needed to be done. I have no idea if it's true but someone told us that one of his assistants was tasked with building a shop, using the leftover materials on the building site. I'm not one to argue with a good story, but don't quote me on this. And so a shop was hurriedly constructed, as a kind of lean-to on the north side of the old cathedral ruins, and not quite opposite the entrance to the new one. It's a very odd shape, echoing the zigzag sides of the cathedral. It has a flat roof and huge, single-glazed windows. Being on the north side of the cathedral, it never gets the sun.

I racked my brains to try and remember what it was like inside. I was sure I had been in there, but not for a long time. It always seemed to be closed. I had a vague feeling it was dark and cold and a bit pokey. I continued to be sceptical. Also, it was the Cathedral's gift shop. We couldn't just turf them out. It turned out that Morris and Naomi, working in the diocesan offices, right next door to the cathedral, had more info on this. Once the initial huge influx of tourists had passed, the shop gradually declined, as it really wasn't in the right place. For a few years it had sat empty, as the Cathedral moved their shop inside, but then there was the problem of having a gradually deteriorating empty building, slap bang between the two beautiful cathedrals, old and new. They reluctantly moved back in, using half the space for cathedral gifts, and the other half rented out to Traidcraft who ran their own shop. Morris seemed very sure that the Dean and Chapter would be delighted if someone came and offered to take on this less than auspicious building. I had my doubts, but was also a little bit excited, and was eager to go and look at the shop as soon as possible.

Persuading the Cathedral

That same evening, we did our first covert recce of the old cathedral gift shop, peering through the large windows and trying to get a sense of what it was like. I think I had been in there before, but not for many years.

A few days later, we finally managed to get inside. The good news was that it was much bigger on the inside than it looked from the outside. It also had a storage room and a tiny kitchenette out the back. The bad news was that it was indeed a very strange shape, and very cold and run down. It felt pretty bleak. But Naomi didn't see it that way. What she saw was potential. One of her many gifts is the ability to transform spaces; if she thought this sad old shop could be turned into a welcoming worship space then I believed her. Morris was right, this was the place for us. Now we just needed to persuade the Cathedral to have us.

Fortunately, we already knew the Dean, and not just from being in the same diocese. He had been the Dean of St John's when we were at theological college, so had known us a long time. We took him out to lunch and shared our vision with him. To his absolute credit, he took us seriously. When people come to me with what seem like crazy ideas, I'm not sure I'm always that gracious. He sent us to meet with the Chief Operating Officer of the Cathedral, who was understandably much more cautious, having never met us before. She had worked very hard to right the Cathedral's finances and wanted to be sure that this wouldn't cost the Cathedral anything, not least as they had no money to put into it. We assured her that we would only come if we could guarantee that our costs were covered, and would pay the same rent to the Cathedral for the building as the Traidcraft shop currently paid.

Persuading the Diocese

We had an idea, we had a building, and we had a kind of far-off blurry vision, but what we now needed was money. And to persuade the diocese to give us money, we needed to get our vision into clear focus.

The next few months were spent writing and rewriting vision documents, painting a picture of what we thought our new church would look like. We hoped to create a new and vibrant community in the central tradition of the Church of England. A place where word and sacrament were held in equal esteem. A place where we could confidently invite those people who had questions, felt like misfits, had been hurt by the Church, or just needed a place to belong. Together we would work out what it meant to be a follower of Jesus, pooling all our wisdom, experience and reading of Scripture. We wanted to be a place that was more about journeying with the big questions than arriving at easy answers. We didn't want people to come to church, we wanted them to be an integral part of a church community, where everyone was loved and valued and heard. Above all else we wanted to create a church that was simple, generous and open. These values were at the heart of everything we wrote and everything we imagined.

Ours was a very different vision from that of HTB, and in hindsight I think that the fact that the diocese was about to invest an enormous amount of money in the city-centre HTB plant was an advantage to us. Funding us, at a fraction of the cost, would help ease the qualms of those who really weren't sure about the HTB plant, and show that the diocese was committed to other models and traditions of the Church of England, and not just big evangelical churches.

We sent the Bishop a copy of our vision document and he in turn gave it to a young intern in the office to ask whether he thought it had merit. We are very grateful that Evan, who years later would become a churchwarden of St Clare's, said yes. The Bishop had some very serious questions and challenges for us, but was on board. There was just one more hurdle. We had to persuade Bishop's Council to fund us.

Morris put together a funding proposal for Bishop's Council that was more far-reaching than we had been imagining. It proposed three years' funding of a full-time stipendiary post including housing. It also proposed a £25,000 set-up grant, which seemed like huge riches to us. We couldn't quite believe that the diocese were prepared to even consider this, and I had a serious dose of imposter syndrome.

Just about a year after our attic conversation, and my first tentative email to the Archdeacon, we went to Bishop's Council to present our proposal. At the time, I was the Chair of the House of Clergy, so was already chairing parts of the meeting. It all felt very strange. The three of us – me, Naomi and Morris – presented the proposal and answered a seemingly endless number of questions. John, the Dean, also answered his fair share of them. There was a palpable sense of excitement in the room. Eventually there were no more questions, and Naomi and I left the meeting, so they could discuss it and vote without us being there.

We spent what felt like an agonizing hour or so (I think it was actually more like 20 minutes) waiting outside. Finally, someone came to fetch us – I don't remember who – giving no indication of what had happened. As we walked back into the room, there was a huge round of applause. The Council had loved our vision, had caught our excitement, and unanimously voted in favour of the funding proposal. It was really happening. We were going to leave the security of our lovely vicarage and wonderful churches, and become pioneers.

Doing church differently

Once we had a building and the funding sorted, we turned our minds to thinking seriously about what our new church might actually be like. By God's grace, before we had even started thinking about church planting, we had planned to have a sabbatical. We had been ordained 16 years and had never had one, and we were blessed that we could take it together. We decided that some of that time would be spent visiting churches which seemed to be a bit like what we were imagining. My first thought was that we had to go to Denver to visit the House for All Sinners and Saints, the church that Nadia Bolz-Weber had planted. However, their website made it clear that they understandably weren't keen on visitors (since the success of Nadia's books they had clearly been a bit overwhelmed by sightseers). It was also a very long and expensive way to go when there was really only one church to visit.

We struggled to find churches in the UK, but after some more research we stumbled on a blog about emerging churches in New York City, which seemed to reflect something of what we were aiming for. This was clearly where we needed to go! We secured a grant from Ecclesiastical Insurance and headed off to the Big Apple to try and find some inspiration.

We were not disappointed. Imagine a church where you dance together in a circle to conclude the service; where you meet in the basement of a Liberal synagogue; where you smile at passers-by through large clear windows; where you eat a meal together as an integral part of the worship; where everyone participates in the sermon; where the music is simple chants and harmonies, taught as you go along; where everyone holds hands as you pray; where the singing is accompanied by a squeezebox or a jazz band; where large numbers of doughnuts and bagels are eaten before and after the service; where children crowd around the communion table; where everyone who comes helps to set things up and clear away; where the Bible reading is interpreted in song and dance; where most of the people present are under 30.

These are just some of the wonderful things we encountered on our tour of exciting and different churches on our sabbatical. There were a few moments when we felt a bit out of our comfort zone (maybe no bad thing), some moments when we felt a bit unsure, but many more moments when we were inspired, encouraged and welcomed. Most of the churches we visited were quite small, and it was a credit to them how graciously they welcomed us into their fellowship.

Our first stop was in London, to visit the Church on the Corner, an Anglican church plant that meets in what used to be a pub, on the corner of a busy road in Islington. They'd been going for 20 years and yet the congregation remained young. They meet on a Sunday evening and when we attended (the Sunday after Easter) it was a lay-led service of the word. The music (a lovely mix of old hymns and contemporary songs) was led by a young woman with a guitar. The vicar appeared from the congregation to give an excellent sermon but that was all. There were the usual refreshments after the service, before a large group of us hot-footed it to the local pub to continue the fellowship. On the face of it there was nothing radical about this church, but it had a freshness, a simplicity and a youthful outlook which we loved. If our new church could look anything like this in 20 years' time, that would be amazing.

We then set off on our transatlantic adventure where we visited four more churches. The first visit was to St Paul's Chapel in the financial district of Manhattan. This beautiful old church (old by American standards, that is – it opened in 1766) used to sit in the shadow of the Twin Towers and was miraculously undamaged when the Towers fell. It's Episcopalian, and part of Trinity Church Wall Street, but has a distinct character of its own. The Sunday morning service is all age, exuberant, eucharistic and only 45 minutes long. When the service was set up a few years ago, this was what the parents at the local school said they wanted. And they come in droves. The church was packed with families eating doughnuts before the service, which began at 9.15 a.m. The priests were robed, there was a full printed order of service and in many senses it was a very traditional 'Anglican' service. But it was also anything but. A child led the priests in, carrying a cross strewn with ribbons. We were seated in the round and the children came and crowded round the priest on a carpet in the centre as she sat to lead a superb all-age sermon. It was Good Shepherd Sunday and we laughed out loud when she asked the children if any of them had ever seen a sheep, assuming it was a joke. But almost none of them had. At communion the children gathered round the table, and everyone was invited to share in bread and wine. A choir of church members led the music (not robed, and sitting together within the congregation), accompanied by the piano.

Refreshments continued after the service, but people seemed to disappear quite quickly, some of them heading to discipleship groups and Sunday School at Trinity. But for others, the reason for the early start was so that they had time to get on and enjoy the rest of the day.

Later that same day, we caught the subway across the East River to Brooklyn to visit our next church, St Lydia's Dinner Church. We were a bit concerned that our visit coincided with their first service without their pastor Emily, who had left for pastures new. It was her vision and drive that established the church 14 years previously, so we were interested to see how they were feeling without her. The church meets in what looks like a shop, with a welcoming A-board outside, reassuring us that we were in the right place. We were welcomed in, then set to work, laying tables and lighting candles, ready for the worship. Other folks were busy in the kitchen. We began at six o'clock, gathering near the door for the opening greeting. As we sang a simple chant, accompanied by a young man playing the squeezebox, we loosely processed to form a large circle around the three tables where we would eat. In the circle we shared in the first part of the Eucharist. The liturgy was sung by the priest, with us joining in with simple chanted responses, and a homemade loaf was shared around the circle. We then sat to eat a delicious meal, including the rest of the bread, and it was clear that our fellowship and conversation was part of the worship. After we'd eaten there was a Bible reading, and the priest (this time Lutheran) gave the sermon, after which he invited comment and discussion from others. We joined hands for a time of open intercession, before standing together for the conclusion of the meal, which was sharing of the wine (though in fact it was grape juice). We were then set tasks to get the washing-up done and the room cleared before we gathered back where we had started for the conclusion. This was when we danced. I was too busy concentrating on not falling over to be self-conscious! The worship was so different from anything I had ever encountered before; an extraordinary mix of very ancient and completely fresh and new. There were only 24 places at the tables, so in order to grow, they now also meet on a Monday night, and once a month have all-age waffle church on a Sunday morning. If we hadn't known about Emily's departure, we wouldn't have been able to tell. They seemed a very happy, active community of young Christians.

We had a week for sightseeing, before heading back to Brooklyn the following Sunday for our third church, Bushwick Abbey, another Episcopalian church. One of the youngest churches we visited, it had been started just a few years earlier, meeting at first in a bar, before moving to a slightly shabby church, which they share with the local Spanish-speaking congregation. The priest who set up Bushwick Abbey left sooner than anyone expected and I suspect she was a hard act to follow. Numbers were low as it was Mother's Day and so many of the regulars were away seeing Mom. The service was quite traditional, but once again, the age profile was young (almost all under 30) and the music very contemporary and original, led by an excellent band. The sermon was loosely based on the model of *Lectio Divina*. The priest read through the passage a couple of times, and we were all invited to share our thoughts. We were really impressed by the theological fluency of the young people, almost all of whom spoke, which surely bodes well for the future of this fledgling church community. After the service we were invited to join them for pancakes and mimosas as they said goodbye to a member who was leaving. Once again, we were made to feel very welcome.

On the Monday evening we made our final visit, this time to a Presbyterian church, the brilliantly named Not so Churchy. Situated just off Broadway, they have a particular calling to people working in the theatres. They meet once a month on a Monday evening, as it's the day when many of the theatres are closed. We had a bit of trouble finding them as, when we reached the address, it seemed to be a synagogue. Eventually, someone appeared at the door on welcoming duty, and we discovered that they meet in a room in the lower floor of this beautiful building. People gathered to chat in the central foyer area, before the worship leader started singing a simple song, which we were soon able to join in with, and we continued to sing as we made our way into the worship space. We sat in the round with the communion table at the centre. The service was highly planned and beautifully delivered with a lot of music and singing, led by immensely accomplished musicians. Meike the priest did surprisingly little of the service, which was very collaborative. Three of the members led the 'Scripture interpretation'. They read a passage from Romans, with quiet background music, periodically swelling as we joined in a simple repeated chant. The sermon was fairly conventional, but once again we were invited to offer our own comments and reflections in response. The service concluded with the sharing of communion, which was banana bread and wine.

Some clear themes emerged as we visited these churches. All make a point of extending a welcome to those who may feel that church is not for them, be it because of their age, their noisy children or their sexuality. All of them managed to be clearly part of the rich tradition they had emerged from, but the worship had been reimagined in order to reach out to younger people in their particular context. We came home with some great ideas and hugely inspired. It felt as if we were beginning to get a sense of what our new church might look like.

Who are we here for?

As we prayed and explored and visited churches, we were honing the vision for our church. We realized that we couldn't be all things to all people. We needed to be clear about who it was we were hoping would come. In general, I don't like the idea of monoculture churches; for me, church should be vibrantly diverse, full of people of all ages, backgrounds and from all types of household. But our calling had come from a desire to reach out to those who were missing from church, so we needed to think about who they were.

There was one group on my mind who were at Lillington, but that was part of the problem. We had a wonderful choir and associated youth group. Young people would move from Sunday Club to singing in the choir, or serving at communion, and most of them were also part of our small but fabulous youth group. This group met once a month and we would play games, read the Bible, talk about faith and pray together. They would sometimes plan and lead services in church. They were committed and faithful members of our church family.

But then somehow, when they left to go to university, as so many of them did, they mostly stopped going to church. Not completely, as they would still come to church at Lillington when they were back for the holidays, but they didn't go to church at university. The habit of churchgoing was soon lost, until eventually church was something they only did at Christmas when visiting Mum and Dad. The problem wasn't a lack of faith or desire, it was finding a church where they felt they belonged. Most student churches are large and evangelical. The style of worship at these churches was completely alien to our young people and the often conservative theology was just not acceptable to them. If they tried going to a church a bit like Lillington there were different issues. They would find that there were no other people their age, and it was hard to fit in. We wanted St Clare's to be a place where young people who grew up attending central churches, who came to Coventry to study or to work, could find a place to belong.

As well as those who had just drifted away from church, often through no fault of their own, there were also the people who had felt they could no longer stay in church for any number of reasons. I was increasingly aware of how many Christians there were who just didn't feel they fitted in any more.

And then there were all the countless people whom I met pretty much every day, who were seeking after something, who had a longing for God, but somehow church as we were doing it didn't quite work for them.

And so we finally put down on paper a vision statement of what we wanted to be.

St Clare's is a small and friendly inclusive church community, that offers a home to the spiritually seeking, to those who have wandered away from God, to those who never knew him and to those who have lost faith in the church.

Hang on!

It wasn't all plain sailing. I spent a lot of time being completely terrified about the prospect of what we were doing, whether we were up to the challenge, and what we would do if the whole thing was a complete failure. Without Naomi's drive and determination, St Clare's would never have come into being, as she kept pushing us to get the next thing done, and to stay on track.

Those months between securing the funding and launching St Clare's felt like being on a rollercoaster, but without the safety bar down, and driven by God. We were so sure this was our calling and it would be OK, but it didn't stop the ride being both exhilarating and terrifying. We just had to hang on and trust that God was in control. We had an incredible sense of God's presence, encouragement and reassurance in it all, more than I have ever experienced in my life. There are numerous stories I could tell of the Spirit's assurance, but these are just a couple of them.

It was late one evening, and for some long-forgotten reason I was in the church at Lillington, possibly locking up after baptism preparation. St Clare's was on my mind. We had told everyone we were leaving, and what the vision was. There was no going back now. The doubts crowded in. What on earth made me think that I could do this, that anyone would come?

I told God how I was feeling. I find chatting out loud to God in quiet, empty churches, when you know you are alone, enormously helpful. Getting to do that whenever you want to is a definite perk of being a vicar. As I did so, I noticed the display board next to the font. It was covered in pictures of smiling children in Malawi, children being helped by a charity that we as a church were supporting. In the middle of one of the pictures, sitting on a motorbike, was a smiling elderly woman. That was Gail, one of our newer members. Gail was a co-founder of the charity. In her retirement, she had gone with two friends to visit Malawi, not knowing that her life was about to be changed for ever. They fell in love with the place and the people, but were hugely moved by the level of need they saw there. They came home determined to set up a charity to help. And they did.

Eighteen years later, that charity continues to help countless people to live healthy, self-sufficient lives.

As I reached the back of the church, I noticed the large box, overflowing with donations of food, toiletries, socks and the like, which we collected for the local night shelter. Mary, another of our members, another woman of more mature years, was one of its co-founders. A few years previously, she had attended a meeting organized by local churches, to talk about the lack of provision for homeless people in the town. There had been a lot of talking, but not a lot of anything getting done. Mary and one other person decided that they would do something. With no experience, and limited support, they determinedly just got on with it, and soon the town had a night shelter.

As I locked the door of the church, I noticed the rota for Sunday, and Jean's name on the list of sidespersons. Jean had been reluctant to join the team, because she was away a lot travelling. Nothing unusual about that, you might think, but Jean hadn't started travelling until she was in her 70s, after being widowed. She had always longed to travel, but it had never been part of her life as a wife, then mother and grandmother. But now, the children were grown up, and her husband had died, so what was stopping her? Nothing. And so she began to travel the world. She has been to the Arctic and the Antarctic, she has climbed in the foothills of the Himalayas, been to all the continents, sometimes travelling alone, sometimes with friends or family. She was the only member of the PCC without email, as why would she spend money on a laptop or internet when she could be putting it towards her next adventure? She is one of the most widely travelled people I know.

Sometimes God is quiet, other times God shouts. 'Come on, Charlotte. If Gail, Mary and Jean can do what they did, and they were all a lot older than you are, then you can do this.' Even now, when I am feeling uncertain about whether I can do something, I take a breath and remember those three ordinary and extraordinary women.

During our sabbatical, as well as the trip to New York, we also spent a week at Minehead at Spring Harvest. A friend of one of Naomi's brothers had a spare room in the luxury apartment he had booked, and very generously offered it to us for free. We knew that we would disagree with much of the theology and teaching, but it was a free week at the seaside, and we were looking forward to the worship and the opportunity for a big sing. The lovely apartment was also a million miles from the cold and run-down chalets I remember from attending Spring Harvest as a teenager.

It was all much as we expected. We got grumpy about a lot of the teaching (or lack of it when it came to Bible study), we enjoyed all the fun of the park and eating chips on the seafront, and we loved the singing. The worship leader was Lou Fellingham, whom we had not come across before, and we loved her. We loved how she would gently remind us of God's grace when, on a couple of occasions, the preacher had forgotten to do so. We loved learning new songs, and in particular we fell in love with one song, which became something of a theme song for us in the months ahead.

As we sang it the first time, with thousands of other people, it absolutely felt like God was speaking directly to us. I went to the shop and bought her CD and put it in the car, playing that one song pretty much on repeat for the next six months. Four lines in particular stood out: 'When we have exhausted our store of endurance, when our strength has failed and the day is half done, when we've reached the end of our earthly resources, our Father's full giving is only begun.'[4]

How true those words have been for us, as at every moment of exhaustion, at every point when we felt entirely inadequate to the task ahead, God has blessed us more.

New central church

There is a large square area, just outside the main door of St Clare's, which is designed for a sign. We needed to swap out the tired old cathedral gift shop sign (they were busy setting up

4 Lou Fellingham, Chris Eaton, Abby Eaton (adapted from Annie Johnson Flint), 2017, 'This Changes Everything', *Everlasting Arms*, Integrity Music.

a lovely new gift shop in the main cathedral itself) for a shiny new St Clare's sign, announcing to the world that we were here. But what to put on our sign? What did we want to convey to people walking past?

We decided to have a picture of St Clare. Naomi set about creating an image of her using lino-cutting, a new craft she had recently discovered, and had a kit and a can-do attitude. We also included the logo that I had designed for us. It includes a large open circle, a symbol of what we were hoping to be; a community in which people can be loved and held, but which is always open to newcomers. Our values are also part of the logo. Simple, generous and open. Finally, we boldly added the words, 'a new central church community'.

From the outset we had a vision of leading a church that was much less bound by tradition and much younger than many Anglican churches. A church rooted in both word and sacrament, with a very contemporary feel, deeply inclusive, and which actively encouraged questioning. A church that didn't define itself as liberal or evangelical but drew from the best of both. In other words, a radically updated version of the often slightly stuffy 'central' church. Central church for the young, as well as for those who had drifted away from church as they found the teaching in evangelical churches too closed but the worship in central or high churches too far from what they were used to.

Most churches in the Church of England would identify in some way with the central tradition, and yet very little in the way of renewal or reform is available to them. New Wine, On Fire, Greenbelt, Walsingham – these all offer encouragement and inspiration to particular groupings within the church, but we struggled to find anything that primarily aims to inspire and encourage central churches, which are probably the majority in the Church of England. At a time in which the ends of the spectrums in the mixed economy of the Church of England are seeking to crystallize their views and positions, we wanted to offer a meeting place where thinking people could wrestle together with what it means to follow Jesus in our world today, without feeling either that they would be told what conclusions to come to, or that they need not fully engage with the Bible and Christian tradition.

This was not simply pragmatism: the central church with its love of word and sacrament had become our spiritual and theological home and we longed to see it reimagined and renewed.

Once the design was finalized, I set about finding a company to make our sign. A week later they arrived to put it up. It was huge. And I mean HUGE. And most of it was Naomi's tiny linocut, blown up about 100 times to over a metre high. It certainly made a statement. We had arrived.

Poor Naomi got the shock of her life leaving work that day. As she exited the front door of the diocesan offices, opposite St Clare's on the other side of a grassy area, she was confronted by her artwork in all its massive glory. She, of course, saw all the 'flaws', but I just think it's amazing, especially as it was her first ever attempt at a linocut.

St Clare's at the Cathedral.
A new central church community.
Simple, Generous, Open.

We were ready to launch.

Not that Rowan Williams

We launched St Clare's on 11 August 2017, St Clare's Day. It felt important to do something to say that we were starting, not least as lots of people from the parishes we had just left were asking about whether there was a service akin to a licensing they could come to. We had actually been licensed by the Bishop a couple of weeks earlier in his chapel at Evening Prayer, and there was no church yet to invite people to, so we decided to have a launch event. St Clare's Day being when it is confirmed for us that she was the right saint.

We weren't quite sure what to do at this event, and eventually decided that I would give a bit of a talk about our vision and what we hoped would happen (and maybe persuade a few folks to sign up as givers). This didn't feel like quite enough, so Naomi came up with the bright idea of inviting someone to come and talk a bit about St Clare. As it turned out, a friend of ours was an expert on St Clare, having recently written a book about her. She would be the perfect person to ask. And so the posters went up, and the emails were circulated.

Come to the St Clare's launch event. Learn what our vision is, eat ice creams, and hear a talk about St Clare from the Revd Rowan Williams.

To be fair to ourselves, we did try and make it clear that this Revd Rowan Williams was a she, but it felt rude and frankly disloyal to make too much fuss about it, such as putting in brackets 'Not the Archbishop, another Rowan Williams', as she is as entitled to the name as he is.

The day arrived and it was wonderful. The sun shone, and lots of the lovely people from Lillington and Old Milverton came to cheer us on. My mum and my sister, who both live a long way away, turned up unexpectedly, which was amazing. People were excited by our vision and fascinated by what Rowan had to say about St Clare. Lots of ice creams were consumed.

I knew almost everyone who was present, but there was one chap, hovering at the back, looking slightly confused, who I didn't recognize, and he didn't seem to be with anyone I knew. I went and spoke to him. It was Rob, owner of a glorious second-hand bookshop in Coventry. He had seen the poster and was very excited about hearing Rowan Williams speak, and right on his doorstep. To his credit, even when he realized it was not *that* Rowan Williams, he stayed and listened, and said he found it all very interesting. Since then we have become friends, as he regularly pops in to look at my books and see if there are any that might make their way from my bookshop to his.

Pete

Just three of us have been part of St Clare's from the very beginning. Me, Naomi and Pete. Pete turned up on week one and was the only person I hadn't previously met or had some inkling might be there. In the terror and excitement of that first Sunday, I don't remember much about any conversation we might have had.

But the next week, Pete was back, and the next and the next and pretty much every week after that. In the early days especially, this was an extraordinary gift. When we set out for St Clare's on a Sunday morning, we could be pretty confident that Pete would be there, even if no one else came. Pete was one of the few people who tramped through the snow to get there on the week when all the roads were closed and the buses stopped because of the weather. Pete was, and is, part of the foundations of St Clare's, helping to keep our community strong and stable.

Pete did not grow up in a Christian home but came to faith as a teenager. On arriving at Warwick University (which is confusingly in Coventry, not Warwick), they went to the campus chapel, and found a community they loved. After graduating, when friends moved away or found other churches, Pete didn't. They found a job in the city and continued to attend the chapel. But after a few years, it was clear that they no longer really fitted there, and so they left, and were adrift.

They heard about St Clare's from someone they knew a bit from an online group they were part of who told them that they planned to come. They invited Pete to join them.

And so Pete turned up. And Pete stayed.

But Pete is so much more than their constancy. I love their wide arms and amazing bear hugs, which they are always so ready to give if you feel in need of one. They are also fascinated by words, and often bring valuable insights to our discussions about the roots of words or other possible translations. When we are uncertain of quite what something means, we always look to Pete.

Pete is kind and funny and highly intelligent. Pete is also autistic, something that they were only formally diagnosed with in the time we have known them. It didn't come as a surprise to us or them but was helpful in giving language to their way of seeing the world. Pete is also non-binary.

But for me, above all else Pete is our rock. Faithful, dependable and strong, Pete gave us confidence right from the beginning that this calling we'd had, this vision for a church for people who don't neatly fit into boxes, this community was real.

Simple

When the Pharisees heard that he had silenced the Sadducees, they gathered together, and one of them, a lawyer, asked him a question to test him. 'Teacher, which commandment in the law is the greatest?' He said to him, '"You shall love the Lord your God with all your heart, and with all your soul, and with all your mind." This is the greatest and first commandment. And a second is like it: "You shall love your neighbour as yourself."' (Matthew 22.34–39)

Keep it simple

I don't like rotas. I'm sure I'm not alone in this, especially among the clergy. Most parish churches are governed by a complex number of rotas ensuring that all the tasks get done on a Sunday. The rota system at Lillington was particularly complex, as there were nearly as many people involved in compiling them as there were rotas. Our parish administrator spent hours and hours nagging people (including me) to get the rotas to her, organizing swaps and filling gaps. I just had a feeling that it didn't need to be quite this complicated or take up quite as much time as it did.

One day I totted them up and discovered that there were no fewer than 12 rotas, just for our main Sunday morning service. There were rotas for the service leader, the preacher, the person doing the Bible reading, the person leading intercessions, the servers, the chalice bearers, the prayers-for-healing team, the sidespeople, the money counters, the coffee makers, the flower arrangers and the Sunday Club leaders. Baptisms and evensong had their own additional rotas.

Some of this had emerged from a commendable desire to ensure that as many laity as possible were involved in the worship and church life in general, as opposed to the priest doing everything, but the level of organization required for a couple of hours on a Sunday morning did at times seem disproportional. If you were starting a church from scratch, surely there was a better way of doing things? Couldn't everything just be a bit more simple?

And not just the number of rotas. It's also about the worship. I am in awe of people who lead beautifully choreographed, complex worship. And when it's done right, it is wonderful, but it's not for me. Leading complicated worship just makes me anxious. And that anxiety can rub off. When I arrived at Lillington I discovered that several of the servers lived in fear of making a mistake in the service. At some point one of my predecessors had so emphasized the importance of worship being perfect, that they lived in dread of getting anything wrong. The day I unthinkingly moved the chalice so the poor young server poured wine onto the carpet was a real breakthrough moment. He froze, a look of absolute horror on his face, assuming that he was going to be in terrible trouble (even though it was entirely my fault). I, by contrast, got the giggles. I couldn't quite believe what an idiot I'd been, and it was quite funny. Then the server started giggling, and we just carried on, hoping that no one had noticed.

Don't get me wrong, worship should be done well, with respect, ensuring that, wherever possible, worshippers are not distracted by those of us with the privilege of leading. For me, that means keeping things simple. I just find complicated worship stressful and that's no good for anyone. It's another reason why I'm a central Anglican. My personal preference is for worship that is simple and ordered and dignified. It's what connects me best to God. It also means I'm less likely to make mistakes, am more relaxed, so lead better. And the better I do my job, the better it is for everyone.

Keeping things simple also means less planning. Over the years, like any jobbing vicar, I have started numerous new services. Midweek communions, all-age services, services at residential and nursing homes, reflective evening services. For some of these, I put together a simple liturgy, and then each week or month, depending on how often it was, just a Bible reading, a homily, some prayers and maybe a hymn needed preparing. If pushed I could lead the service with almost no preparation. By contrast, other services involved a whole team of people who met to discuss and individually craft each service. These high-input services were often extraordinary, especially at the outset. But they were not sustainable. Very soon, it became hard to find time to meet together, ideas were harder to generate, and I ended up doing most of the planning. In time, the service always began to feel like a burden rather than a gift.

When we started thinking about what the worship at St Clare's should look like, we kept this in mind. We wanted worship that we could lead with confidence. Starting a whole new church was terrifying enough, without the added pressure of complicated worship to worry about. And it also needed to be simple to create, so that it could be put together week by week, without needing too much time or coordination. As two pioneers, one with a full-time job, and the other figuring out how to run a shop to pay for everything, we didn't have time to spend crafting complicated or bespoke worship each week. We wanted to invest the time we had into relationships and creating community.

We have the same liturgy every week, the Church of England communion service, but stripped down to essentials. When you look carefully at the rubrics, there is quite a lot that is optional. We sit in a circle – there's no processing, or worrying too much about when to stand up, sit down or move around. We have no rotas (though we do have a service plan) and each week we just ask the question, 'Who would like to read the Bible reading?' On more than one occasion, it has been a newcomer on their first visit to us who has enthusiastically offered.

What's in a name?

I have to confess that visiting the churches was pretty much all the research I did about setting up a pioneer church community. I had been put off by reading a Grove booklet on the subject, which made it clear that we were going about it in all the wrong way. However, we did agree with its certainty that any new church must have a name. A name is what gives something identity, and it can imbue meaning and purpose. A name also makes you simple to identify. If you know my name, you know who I am.

So how to choose a name? The first bit was easy. We were starting an Anglican church, and Anglican churches are named after saints, so we just needed to find the right one. Naomi then had the idea that perhaps we should choose one of those represented in the great glass west screen of the cathedral just outside our building. But they were mostly men, and it made us realize that we'd really like it to be a female saint. The Cathedral is dedicated to St Michael, so it would even things out. We loved the idea of St Lydia, that pioneering businesswoman and church leader, but it felt as if we would be copying the idea from St Lydia's Dinner Church.

And so, one evening, we got out the illustrated book of saints that was on our bookshelves and started reading through it, hoping to be inspired. It didn't take long. The saints were listed in alphabetical order and we only got as far as C. The second we read about St Clare of Assisi we knew she was the one.

The first thing that appealed (and made us laugh) was that she was the patron saint of needleworkers. By now, we had started to develop the idea of running a shop alongside the church, and Naomi, who had become a highly competent dressmaker over the last couple of years, was thinking about sewing clerical shirts to sell. We read on and discovered that Clare was a pioneer, who founded and led her own order, and was the first woman to be allowed to write a rule of life for her community. She sounded like our kind of gal! She was also the patron saint of television, which also seemed appropriate for us, as people who do enjoy watching telly. We did read on to the end of the book of saints, but truth be told we knew from the moment we got to her that it was to be St Clare's.

Travel light

For many years, I was very proud of the fact that all my worldly goods would fit into my car. This gave me a sense of freedom, albeit a false one. I hated the idea of being tied down, of being trapped, and liked knowing that, if I wanted to, I could quit my job, pile everything I owned into my car and hit the road. I obviously hadn't thought through where I would sleep or how I would afford to live, but the idea of it gave me a sense of peace.

Once I arrived at theological college, I gradually began to accumulate stuff, and by the time I arrived at Lillington, nine years later, Naomi and I had enough 'stuff' to fill a large four-bedroomed vicarage with an enormous garden, garage and outbuildings.

When we got the go-ahead for St Clare's, for the first time in 20 years we were moving into smaller accommodation. A lot smaller. As well as the generous set-up grant, the diocese had provided church housing. We didn't need a full-sized vicarage and were more than delighted with a small three-bed semi, just a mile from the cathedral. But it did mean major downsizing. We think we probably got rid of half of everything we owned, which was a hugely time-consuming and exhausting business. But it also felt exciting. We were going to be pioneers, heading off into the unknown, and we didn't want to be weighed down by too much baggage.

We also needed to get rid of a huge amount of church baggage that we had gathered over the years. If we tried to carry all the complexity, tradition and ways of doing things from church as we knew it, we would quickly collapse under the weight of it. Keeping things simple stops us getting bogged down in things that might distract us from our vision. We regularly try new things, but if something is becoming overly complicated, or isn't working, we don't just keep piling more and more effort in, we just stop it.

One Sunday in our worship we were discussing the story of Philip and the Ethiopian Eunuch in Acts 8. One of our members commented that thinking about Philip challenged her to 'be more nimble'. Quicker to respond to the callings of the Spirit, to the situations around us, to new ideas, places and conversations. It's much easier to be nimble when you aren't weighed down with more than you need. A constant question at St Clare's is, 'Do we need to be carrying this?' It's a question I wish I'd asked a lot more in my previous parishes, and even more, wish I'd been braver in stopping things sooner than I did.

Early on at St Clare's, we decided to start a monthly board-game evening. Board-game cafés were popping up all over the place, and lots of us were board game fans, so it seemed a good thing to do. But in the end it wasn't fun. It was a lot of hard work for me, and for a number of reasons didn't really work as we'd hoped. And so we stopped it. It felt like failure. But it wasn't, no more than a toddler learning to walk fails when they fall over. It just wasn't the right thing for us, and I had to learn that it was OK for things not to work. We have started and stopped numerous initiatives in our seven years. Some things just didn't work. Some things worked for a while, but then didn't. If it's not working, we just stop it. No drama, no agonizing over why it didn't succeed. Just some reflection on what we need to take with us from the experience before moving on to the next thing.

A few things well

Keeping things simple also helps us to stay outward looking. The more complicated church becomes, the more likely it is that we are putting so much time and energy into running church, that we aren't spending time on building community, deepening relationships and growing the kingdom in the wider world.

'Do a few things well' was an almost constant mantra of Bishop Colin, Bishop of Coventry when I was first ordained. He was always encouraging churches to do less, and to do it better. He's not wrong, but it's very hard to believe that it is really

OK when you look at all the amazing things your neighbouring church is apparently doing, or hear tales of seemingly endless social action projects, courses and services from your fellow clergy at chapter meetings.

This pressure increased during my time at Lillington as, with a new bishop, I noticed a subtle but definite change in how churches operated. This change was driven partly by Morris, the Archdeacon, and partly in response to the needs of the country around us. There was increasingly an expectation that churches should be heading up significant projects. Of course, many churches, especially in the areas of greatest need, had already been doing this, but it was generally the exception rather than the rule. All churches offered support to charities and good causes, but now the churches were *becoming* the charities and good causes. Food banks, debt advice centres, work clubs and drop-ins began to pop up in churches all around us. I was disconcerted about this. I didn't have the skills, the calling or the capacity to get a new thing up and running, and wasn't really sure I thought it was the right thing for us to be doing anyway, but couldn't put my finger on quite why. I was also unsure whether enough people in church had the time or energy to take on a big new social action project. We already ran an After School Bible Club, which (being the only free club) attracted the children most in need, and that was hard enough.

I was pondering on this when I came to write my Maundy Thursday sermon that year, thinking about Jesus washing his disciples' feet, a humble and generous act of service, and wondering what it meant for us at Lillington.

I started to think about the acts of service that people in our church were already involved in. I started to make a list of charities that I knew people from church volunteered for. Within a couple of minutes I had jotted down 15 organizations, and those were just the ones I could immediately bring to mind, or even knew about. I also knew that many of the church members were exemplary in caring for infirm neighbours, visiting, shopping and cooking for them. We also had two local councillors in the church, who served the community in that way. Then there were those who poured time and love into the church itself, to make sure that the building and the churchyard were beautiful and welcoming spaces.

It made me realize that my personal ecclesiology is that of church as primarily a place of community, growth and mutual support, from which members go out into the wider world, taking the love of Christ into workplaces, volunteering, and everything else they do, as salt and light. It's not that the church does nothing corporate (at Lillington we ran not only the After School Bible Club but also a toddler group, a small charity for people in need in the community and a weekly 'tea and chat' for older folks), but that isn't our main purpose. From the moment of writing that sermon, I resisted calls for us to do more church corporately, but also made sure that we celebrated, supported and encouraged people in their various acts of service.

This feels even more important in St Clare's, where everyone is of working age. We have teachers, charity workers, social workers, engineers and students, as well as new mums and those unable to work. No one really has the time to be involved in additional projects run by the church. And so we don't do them. Instead, we offer our beautiful space for free to charities who might find it useful, and I do an enormous amount of pastoral care in the shop week by week. And everyone is living out their calling to be a disciple of Christ in some way or another beyond the church community, whether in the workplace, volunteering, or simply in their love and care for others around them. And we celebrate and support one another in that.

Marginal gains

At the 2012 London Olympics, the British cycling team dominated their field, winning pretty much everything. As if this isn't astonishing enough, what is even more amazing is that prior to the 2008 Olympics they had won only one gold medal in the previous 100 years.

So what changed?

In 2003 a new performance manager was hired, Dave Brailsford. He brought a new strategy to the team, which he referred to as 'the aggregation of marginal gains'. His theory was that rather than trying to improve things by making big definable changes, maybe focusing on a couple of areas, instead try and improve everything you do by a tiny amount.

I loved the idea of this. It felt as if it gave a name and a value to what I was already instinctively doing. I have never been one for making big changes. In clergy circles you hear so many stories of new vicars going in and making massive changes to a church, often leaving the people floundering in the wake. Sometimes it works, but usually at a significant cost.

Sometimes big changes are necessary and unavoidable. Eventually we couldn't keep patching up the heating system at Lillington, so it had to be replaced. But with the things that are going OK, or even going well, it can be tempting just to leave well alone, adopting a very sensible 'if it's not broke, then don't fix it' attitude. But that's how things get tired and stale and start to lose their effectiveness. Trying to keep adjusting and improving the things that are going OK makes sure we continue to thrive and grow.

On the face of it, the Sunday worship at St Clare's looks pretty much the same as it did when we started seven years ago. But look more closely and you see that there have been quite a lot of changes. We have constantly been adjusting things, in response to the community and as we reflect on what is working well, and what isn't, and find ways to slightly change things to improve them.

The music is a good example of this. When we started St Clare's, we made no attempt to include corporate singing. We didn't know if we had any musicians, live music is very complicated to organize, and we also thought it might prove awkward or embarrassing with a very small group of people.

We did however include music in the service, played through our highly sophisticated sound system … a Bluetooth speaker! It's a very good Bluetooth speaker but cost just £150 rather than many thousands of pounds. We had a piece of music at the beginning, to help us to focus and settle, ready for worship. And then we would have another piece of music as we received communion. We might also have another piece for reflection or during the intercessions.

The music we included varied, and I quickly worked out what did and didn't work in the space. Big guitar-based worship songs didn't work, folk music did. Taizé chants were great, organ music was not. Bit by bit, I adapted and improved our repertoire as I noticed what people responded well to, and what they didn't. We used chants, Christian songs, secular songs, instrumental music, a bit of everything. Sometimes the communion music would be a hymn, and one Sunday we listened to 'Amazing Grace'. As the bread and wine was passed around the room, I noticed that people were beginning to sing. The words and melody were familiar enough that people could join in. Suddenly, there was a profound sense of the Holy Spirit among us, as we worshipped together in song. It was beautiful.

The following week I chose another familiar hymn, and this time printed the words on the weekly sheet. People sang. Singing a hymn or worship song is now part of our weekly service. There was no big change or decision to do it, we just got there as we reflected on what was happening and made small adjustments.

A family that eats together ...

I distinctly remember the moment when I discovered how wonderful purple sprouting broccoli is.

It was a Sunday and we were at Auntie Chris and Uncle Roger's house for lunch. This was something we did regularly but not often, heading off after church on the half-hour drive to the tiny hamlet in the New Forest where they lived. Depending on how many other family members were there, tables would be pushed together in the dining room, and we would all squash in, ready to share the feast. Lunch was always a traditional roast. Every vegetable on the plate had been lovingly grown by Uncle Rog, and prepared and cooked by Auntie Chris. I can't remember how old I was, but that day as my plate was passed to me, it was clear that I was now considered old enough to have the same food as the grown-ups. And there on my plate, looking as unappealing as anything can to a child, was this strange purple-tinged vegetable looking not quite like anything I had seen before. We started eating. I worried about the purple thing. I knew it was impolite to just leave it, but really didn't want to eat it. At some point my mum, as mums do, quietly said I should at least just try it …

I took a tentative mouthful and from that moment purple sprouting broccoli has been my favourite vegetable. Of course it has never since been quite as good as that first taste. But that's not surprising really. It was home grown and freshly picked just a few hours before we ate it.

St Clare's is a eucharistic community, and unapologetically so. Meals are where community is formed, where all ages come together, where there is love and laughter, and where strangers can quickly become friends. At meals we are nourished physically and emotionally, and as we share together we learn and grow. It was at mealtime, Jesus said, that we should remember him and receive afresh his love and healing and strength. And so St Clare's was always going to be centred on a meal, both the symbolic meal that we call Holy Communion, or Eucharist or Mass, but also a real meal, where community could quickly grow.

On Sunday 10 September 2017 we held our first service. We thought long and hard about what time to go for and decided on midday. We hoped to attract students so wanted to make sure it was late enough for them to make it. Truth be told, I was also quite excited about Sunday morning lie-ins, having spent the last decade doing eight o'clock communions.

But by far the most significant reason was so that after the service we could eat together. In our own lives and in the church communities we visited on sabbatical, we had experienced the power of sharing a meal to create and bond community.

Having an actual meal seems to enable relationships to grow in a way that coffee after the service just doesn't, however hard you try. When we were at theological college, we attended lots of different churches, either on placement or for one-off visits. All of them had refreshments after the service and, however hard I tried, I always seemed to find myself standing awkwardly alone, trying to drink a scalding cup of tea or coffee as quickly as I could so that I could leave. This would usually have been preceded by a bit of small talk with one or two keen people, but they soon drifted off to their familiar groups, and I was just left there, wondering whether to try and 'break in' to one of the huddles.

Somehow, if you are eating an actual meal, this doesn't happen as much. Maybe it's because everyone is sitting down. Maybe it's because you're not thinking about rushing home to put the roast on. Maybe it's because eating gives you something to do if no one is talking to you so you don't feel as exposed. Maybe it's just because meals are where communities are formed.

On that first Sunday morning, I got up early and slaved away cooking a large rice salad to accompany bread and cheese and various other bits and pieces. Naomi, unaware that I had been doing this, was horrified. It was week one, and I had already gone against our value of keeping things simple. As Naomi rightly pointed out, we couldn't possibly sustain cooking at this level every week. It would soon become an intolerable burden.

The following week we purchased a soup kettle and served Heinz tomato soup with bread and cheese. One of our youngest members, then aged just three, took to calling it St Clare's soup, and soon we all did. Sometimes people would bring other things to add to the meal, but the basic fare was always the same. Very quickly, the small and diverse group of people who had started joining us on Sundays began to become one community, spending an hour or so together after the worship, getting to know one another, checking in on how they were, and even discussing the sermon. The food didn't need to be fancy. It just needed to be there.

Since the pandemic, we have slightly changed things, and people now bring their own sandwich or the like, though there are always plenty of snacks and drinks available. We had initially planned to return to bread and soup once the concerns and restrictions around shared meals were lifted, but actually it works really well and is even simpler than soup. So for now at least, we're sticking with it.

Sharing a Eucharist every week does mean, in the Church of England, that you need a priest, but the vision for the many new worshipping communities that the Church of England aspires to is that they are primarily led by lay people. This makes a lot of sense in theory, as there are many lay people with the skills and experience to lead new worshipping communities, and priests are increasingly thin on the ground. But leading a new worshipping community – leading any worshipping community – is a vocation. It comes from calling, not just happening to have the right skill set. And in the Church of England, it is as priests where that calling is most often lived out. Those who feel called to lead new worshipping communities are very often also called to priesthood. It is our priests who receive most training, and it is our priests who have both the support and accountability that comes with being ordained.

But it's more than that. For me, the Eucharist is at the heart of our worship. It's the place where we come and receive the grace of God, physically placed into our open hands. It's the family meal of the church. It's where we grow and learn. It's where tentative strangers and tiny children stretch out their hands to receive Jesus. They may not fully understand what it is they are doing, just as I didn't understand how wonderful purple sprouting broccoli was until I tried it, but they cannot know if it isn't offered to them. And I confess that I never ask if people are baptized or confirmed or have any concept of quite what it is they are doing. If their hands are out, they receive bread. To refuse them would be like inviting someone to Sunday lunch and then not letting them eat until they have completed a test to show that they understand the nutritional value of the food. If a meal is at the heart of our worship, then anyone who is present should be fed.

And so I think we should be bolder in our vision. We should enable existing priests and train new ones to lead new worshipping communities. And if there aren't enough, then maybe it should be priests who are sent out to be pioneers, while the gifted and capable laity lead the established communities.

Small is beautiful

One of the questions I am most commonly asked about St Clare's is 'How many people do you get?'

Early on in our journey towards St Clare's, the Bishop had challenged us to think about how we would grow, and we started thinking about whether growth could equate to more than 'bums on seats', which sadly seems to be the metric that people are most interested in.

The worship space in St Clare's is small, so we began to imagine a church that never grew beyond the number of seats available; that wasn't just trying to get more people in, but was also focused on sending them out. We wanted a church with lots of young people. And young people move. They head off to study, or graduate, get new jobs, go travelling. We decided that we would absolutely not try to hang on to people, or be disappointed when the time came for them to leave us. Whether they'd been with us three weeks, three months or three years, we would try hard to send them off with thanksgiving and encouragement, celebrating their time with us. When appropriate we would help them to find a new church community, knowing they would be taking something of the essence of St Clare's with them.

Over the last seven years I have lost count of how many people have been part of our community, for a longer or shorter time. But I do know that there have never been more than 40 active members, and we usually have no more than 20 people on any given Sunday.

I'm trying really hard to be OK with that. Partly for practical reasons. You can get 30 people into our worship space at a push, but ideally you wouldn't want more than 25. We are open to the possibility of moving to a bigger space if needed, but right now that doesn't seem to be what God is calling us to. It would radically change the character of the community, and we wouldn't want to make that jump unless we were really sure it was the right thing to do.

It's also for ecclesiological reasons. Over the years I have been ordained I have more and more come to believe in small churches. It's so easy to get lost in a big church. Especially if you are someone who feels they don't quite fit in. The bigger a group, the more difficult it is to be a bit different. We are blessed with several members with autism at St Clare's. At least one of them came to us having felt completely unseen at her previous church. Big churches work for some people, but often not for those on the edges, or who don't quite fit the norm, or who are particularly struggling with life.

Small means you can build relationships fast and everyone knows each other. There is no need for separate home groups, which a lot of people struggle to commit to, as we can do that community-building work in our worship and over lunch. We do have evening meetings and Bible studies, and people pop into the shop for a chat (with me or with each other), but it's all the same people, deepening their relationships, rather than being in separate cells.

Pastoral care is more manageable, partly because there are literally fewer people, but also because of the way the community supports one another. They don't all look to the vicar for help. I am also more available than many clergy, as you can just come and find me during shop hours. I love how often members of the community come in for a chat on their day off, between lectures or on a lunch break.

Sadly, I don't think the pressure or desire to grow churches numerically is always for the good of the kingdom. Financial pressures make a difference. The more people you have, the more likely you are to be able to pay for the vicar and the upkeep of the building. Would we do church any differently if we never had to worry about the money to pay for it?

And as anyone who has ever been part of a clergy chapter meeting knows, there is status attached to the size of your church. None of us like to admit it, but the truth is that the bigger your church congregation, the more successful you are perceived to be. I have to constantly talk myself down from feeling inadequate when people ask about our numbers. I truly believe that small is beautiful, but that's a hard truth to hang on to in a church obsessed with numbers.

Go outdoors

This ability to be more nimble that simplicity brings came into its own when the pandemic hit. Like most people, I had never heard of Zoom at the beginning of March 2020, but by the end of the month, that's how our weekly worship was being conducted. It worked really well for us, as we were a small enough community for everyone to continue to join in. We added a 'How's it going?' session at the Peace, so everyone who wanted to could let us know how they were doing. Students and others who had gone back to parents for lockdown were able to continue to be part of the community, and whether you were in Coventry, Croydon or even Bangalore (where one of our regular Zoom attenders lives), it made no difference.

When George Floyd was murdered and the Black Lives Matter movement really took off, we were privileged to hear the thoughts of two young black women in our community. Despite being physically separated, those services in early lockdown were some of the most meaningful we had ever had.

It wasn't perfect, though. We had a couple of people who just disappeared, unwilling or unable to join us via Zoom. We were also very aware that once normality returned, a good number of our members would not. One couple would soon be getting married and planned to move to London, a couple of students graduated, others were looking for new jobs. They were all still with us on Zoom, but would not be with us when the pandemic was over. This was fine and normal, people leaving is a normal and celebrated part of our church life, but usually there are also people arriving, and during lockdown they were not.

And so, as soon as it was possible, we returned to in-person worship. Outside.

Coventry is an extraordinary city with an incredible history, going back centuries. However, the destruction of the cathedral, and much of the city, by the Luftwaffe in November 1940 has so dominated our story (and rightly so) that the earlier history of Coventry as a hugely important medieval city has sometimes been a bit neglected.

One thing I always enjoy telling visitors is that we're actually on our third cathedral. We have the magnificent new building, a phenomenal testament to post-war ambition and architecture, completed in 1962. We also have the preserved ruins of the cathedral destroyed in the war, which, although a medieval building, had only been a cathedral for 22 years, given cathedral status when the new diocese of Coventry was established at the end of the First World War.

But long before then, back in the twelfth century, there was previously a diocese of Coventry, and it had a huge cathedral. So huge and so powerful that, come the dissolution of the monasteries, Henry VIII made an example of it, and it was the only cathedral to be entirely dismantled, alongside its Benedictine priory. Just the foundations remain of this vast building, parts of which can still be seen.

Next to the new cathedral, and just opposite St Clare's, there is a lovely area called Unity Lawn. It was originally part of the old cathedral churchyard, but no longer has any gravestones, and is most famous for briefly containing a tree planted by John Lennon and Yoko Ono, as a symbol of peace, before it was dug up by an over-enthusiastic fan.

It's a place surrounded by churches on all sides. To the east is the new cathedral, to the south is the ruined cathedral (and also St Clare's), to the west is Holy Trinity, another large medieval church, and to the north, buried under a row of Georgian houses, are the remains of that first cathedral, St Mary's.

In the summer of 2020 we decided to restart 'in person' on Unity Lawn. The very first Sunday we gathered there, under the shade of the sycamore tree, we knew it was holy ground. There was something deeply mystical about being there, spread out in a wide circle, with two metres between each other, yet sharing communion. Creation joined in our worship. We had to pause the service one Sunday as a massive row broke out between the resident peregrines and seagulls, and we couldn't hear ourselves over the racket. One week, an emboldened great tit came and pinched a piece of Naomi's sandwich from her hand. The squirrels were always close by, hoping for a crisp or some other morsel.

During that summer we were often joined by passers-by.

Some came just once, others for a few weeks. Some people became members of St Clare's and are still with us. It was our small size and the simplicity of what we do that enabled us to make the move, and it was such a blessing. It didn't rain one single Sunday that summer and we worshipped outside right through until the end of September when the cold finally drove us inside.

The following year we thought we'd do the same again, just because it was so lovely. But we hadn't factored in the bell-ringers, who had been absent the previous year. They start ringing at pretty much the same time as we start worshipping. When we are inside it provides a lovely backdrop. Outside it made worship pretty much impossible. In the end we had to admit that the summer of 2020 had been a one-off gift. God's gift of that holy place when we really needed it.

Thinking outside the box

We were very excited when in spring 2018 we had two young people wanting to be baptized. Our first adult baptisms. They really wanted full immersion.

There was clearly no way that was possible inside St Clare's, there just wasn't enough space; so how and where to do it in a way that still felt faithful to St Clare's but was possible and practical?

After thinking about various options, we finally decided to do the service in the cathedral ruins, right next to St Clare's. The next decision was what to use for the baptism. The Cathedral owned a large baptism pool but people in the know told us it was a nightmare to put up, took an eternity to fill, and was almost impossible to get warm. The young woman being baptized was quite nervous about water, and we thought that if the water was properly warm it would be much less traumatic.

We thought about buying something. What we needed was a large water pool that was easy to put up, easy to heat and not prohibitively expensive. If only someone had designed such a thing. Which of course they have. Naomi, who is always able to think outside the box, suddenly declared that what we needed was an inflatable hot tub. Surprisingly affordable, the manufacturers of inflatable hot tubs really could do well marketing them to churches as baptistries.

So it was that on a lovely Saturday evening in spring 2018, we found ourselves erecting a hot tub in the ruins of a medieval cathedral. It takes a while to fill with water, so while we waited, one of us went and got chips and we sat and ate them, perched on an ancient tomb, in that ancient place, in the heart of the city we love.

As we ate, the Dean and his wife walked past, all dressed up in black tie and fancy frock, heading to a function at the Guild Hall in the next street. They looked at us and smiled as we sat chatting to one another, eating our chips in the quiet while they headed off to a noisy event full of small talk and expectations. We laughed at the diversity of ministry, and felt content at the roads not taken.

Once the tub was filled, we put the lid on, turned the heater on, locked the gates of the ruins and left it to warm up, ready for the next day.

The service was completely joyous and the hot tub was an absolute triumph. It wasn't perfect (the bells were very noisy), but perfection isn't what we are aiming for. Authenticity, community and helping people to encounter God are what we are about, and all those things were present in abundance.

Holly

Holly joined us on week three, along with me, Naomi and Pete, the smallest our congregation has ever been. I tried hard not to seem embarrassed or to make excuses for the lack of people. The service included an interactive activity with the prayers and I was pleased that Holly joined in, but was slightly concerned that she seemed to be crying.

She told me later that the few people had been a gift for her. Having been a Christian her whole life, she hadn't been to church for five years, having left the church she'd been part of for many years after her marriage fell apart. People were kind and sympathetic for a while, but eventually she started to feel that there was a time limit on her grief and people were getting fed up with her misery. It seemed to challenge their theology, which assumed that God should have sorted her out by now. And so she left.

Then the week after we opened, she walked past St Clare's and read the vision statement in our window. As she was pondering on this, her phone rang. It was Emma, one of the women who had joined us on week one. She was ringing to tell Holly about St Clare's, thinking that maybe it might be a good place for her to give church another go. This so clearly seemed to be a God thing that she came along the next week, and then the week after that, and then pretty much every week after that. She would sometimes be joined by her teenage daughter, Leanne, who has special needs. One day, Holly nearly fell off her chair in astonishment when Leanne prayed out loud, thanking God for her mum.

Holly was such a gift to us. Despite all that she'd been through, she always seemed to ooze sunshine. She has a radiant smile and a gift for making people feel safe and loved. She also seemed to know everyone in the city. Pretty much everyone who popped into the shop or came to church already knew Holly. This meant that very quickly lots more people knew about us, as word spread through her extraordinary labyrinth of networks. Holly volunteered at the local art gallery and was soon also volunteering in the shop a couple of days a month. We became friends and would regularly walk our dogs together.

In September the following year we were celebrating St Michael and All Angels. We talked about different types of roles that angels in the Bible have, and during a time of quiet, people were invited to 'choose' an angel. I had prepared Bible verses rolled into tiny scrolls in baskets next to each angel for people to take and read. I had hoped that people might find some encouragement or solace from the verses; I hadn't imagine it would change someone's life.

I asked if anyone wanted to share anything. Almost immediately Holly blurted out that she was moving to Devon. We knew this. She'd been talking about it for a while. She had a sister who lived there who needed support, and also thought a fresh start might be good, for her and for Leanne who was really struggling with life. She'd been thinking that maybe she'd go in a year's time when Leanne finished school. But no, she didn't mean that. She meant she was going now. The Bible verse she had picked up was Exodus 23.20, 'I am going to send an angel in front of you, to guard you on the way and to bring you to the place that I have prepared.' As she read it, she powerfully sensed God saying to go now. And so she did. Just a month later, she and Leanne had sold their house, packed up their lives and were ready to go.

We gave them a proper send-off, designing a liturgy of 'sending on', which we still use when people leave. It was bittersweet. We were so sad to lose her but knew that in Holly the vision that God had given us for St Clare's had been fulfilled. She is now settled and happy with a new church and a new relationship. Watching God working his slow and gentle healing in her was a beautiful thing, and she was such a gift to us.

Generous

While he was at Bethany in the house of Simon the leper, as he sat at the table, a woman came with an alabaster jar of very costly ointment of nard, and she broke open the jar and poured the ointment on his head. (Mark 14.3)

Be more generous

My first incumbency was at Potters Green, a small parish in the north of Coventry built in the 1960s, including the church. Naomi was working as a chaplain at an FE college in Nuneaton, earning a pittance. We had just scraped together all our savings to buy a cottage in the valleys of South Wales. I had been to a chapter meeting a few months earlier and the weeping and gnashing of teeth from clergy about to retire and with no home to go to had persuaded us to get on the housing ladder now. Though the cottage had cost a very modest £71,500, paying the mortgage each month was still a challenge. We were reluctant to let it out, however (not that it was in any fit state at that stage), and were enjoying having a place to go to when we had a couple of days off.

One Sunday, after church, we decided to treat ourselves and go out to lunch. Nowhere fancy, just to the Frankie and Benny's up the road at the nearby out-of-town shopping centre. Not long after we'd ordered, a group of young people came in whom we recognized. They were from 'Neighbours and Nations', a house church that met in the parish. I had met the couple who ran it at ecumenical things, but didn't know them well. They smiled and waved. We smiled and waved back. If I'm honest, part of me was a little bit grumpy. If that group of young people, all in

their 20s and 30s, came to St Philip's, it would be transforma-
tional for us. Instead, they had chosen to set up a new church,
meeting in one another's homes (I had no idea that in 12 years'
time, we would do a similar thing).

We finished our meal and called the waitress over to ask for
the bill. 'Nothing to pay,' she said, 'the people at the table over
there have covered it.' She pointed to the table where the group
from 'Neighbours and Nations' were sitting.

This random act of kindness was so appreciated, and we
were deeply touched. We thanked them and left with a spring
in our steps.

A small act of generosity can make a really big difference,
and we began consciously to try and 'be more generous' whenever we could. It became for us a bit of a household motto.
Nothing huge, but just trying to do those small things which
would hopefully make other people feel as blessed as we did
that day in Frankie and Benny's.

When we started St Clare's, 'generous' became one of our
values.

St Clare's was born out of generosity: the generosity of the
diocese in giving us the funding to get started; the generosity
of the Cathedral in welcoming us into the space; the generosity
of friends who came and laboured with us to get the building
ready. We were overwhelmed by the generosity and support of
so many that allowed us do this crazy thing, and we wanted to
pay it forward.

Clergy often describe themselves as being a 'Jack of all Trades'
as we are expected to know way more than how to preach
and lead a service and other more obvious 'vicaring' things.
Depending on your context, you may also have to understand
finance, various aspects of the law, heating systems, how to
look after ancient buildings, grounds maintenance, marketing,
sound systems, church music, fundraising, events management
… the list is endless. In my experience, God can and will use
every tiny bit of talent or experience you have in their service.
As pioneer ministers, especially at the outset, when you are
pretty much on your own, this is even more true.

As well as creating and nurturing a new community, we

would need to be the builders, interior designers, decorators, planners, buyers, designers and manufacturers for St Clare's. For two people who both love turning our hand to a bit of everything, this was exhilarating. To be able to give generously of all our talents to our ministry was and is such a gift.

Three weeks

It wasn't until the middle of July 2017 that we were finally given the keys to the building that would be St Clare's. We'd already told lots of people that we would be launching on St Clare's day, 11 August. We had just three weeks to transform a tired and somewhat neglected building into a warm and hospitable space, ready to open our doors. Without the incredible generosity of friends, we would never have been ready to launch.

It's amazing what you can achieve in three weeks with hard work, and love.

The vision for the building had grown with our vision for St Clare's. We wanted a space that people would feel confident in, even eager to walk into; that inspired interest and curiosity; that looked like a friendly, safe place to enter. During our sabbatical, we were reminded how daunting it can be to take that first step through the doors of an unknown church. If we – a pair of seasoned priests – found it hard, how much trickier for a tentative explorer.

We felt blessed that the building has large plate glass windows (not quite such a blessing in the depths of winter!) so people can see in. We have gone from drab white to rich, warm colours, with things to look at and comfy seating. One end of the building is the worship space. The other end is the shop, and when you come through the door, it's the shop you walk into. This was deliberate. Anyone can walk into a shop. That's what you're supposed to do.

It was a tremendous amount of hard work. We took down old fixtures and built new ones. We painted endless swathes of wall, ceiling and woodwork. We scrubbed, sanded and drilled. We negotiated with the contractors doing the bits we just couldn't manage ourselves, all the while making friends with all our new colleagues at the Cathedral, who seemed amazed and bemused in equal measure by our efforts.

We were deeply touched that friends from absolutely every place we'd previously ministered in the diocese showed up to help us. There were also people we had never met before. On day two in the building, we had a painting party. Ten of us set to with rollers and brushes and got a first coat of paint on at least part of every wall. Another friend gave two whole days each week to come and help. Other friends turned up to do more painting, plumbing and sorting of books, or simply to offer encouragement in what we were doing.

We felt so surrounded and upheld by love. The love of friends and, of course, the love of God. We received unnumbered blessings and loved every minute of the challenge.

St Clare of Assisi said, 'Love God, serve God; everything is in that.' We wrote this in large gold letters on the wall above the communion table. God blessed us with a vision and, in serving God and beginning to make the vision a reality, we had fun. More fun than we could ever have guessed. We almost had to pinch ourselves that it was real.

And so the transformation of the building was done. Ahead was the really daunting part. To start growing a church community; to start being a place where people can come as they are, and find that love which nurtures and transforms; to turn our bricks and mortar into the living, breathing body of Christ.

Tentmakers

While he was in Corinth, Paul worked as a tentmaker (Acts 18). This was presumably to pay his way but was also a means in which he could be a part of the community he had joined, working with them, offering the skills he had for the common good, as well as sharing the gospel. We too had to be tentmakers. Not literal tentmakers, of course (though I'm sure Naomi could work out how to do that if she had to), but metaphorical tentmakers.

In parish ministry, meeting people is easy. There are the people who come to you for baptisms, weddings, funerals, carol services, church fetes. The possibilities are endless. Then there are the people whom you can go to in your role as a vicar: schools, nursing homes, council meetings. These are where the relationships are formed which so often lead to an invitation to church. I quickly realized that I had no idea how to meet people as a pioneer minister. A foray into any of the above would be stepping on the toes of clergy colleagues and I had no intention of doing that. There were plenty of people to go round, we just had to work out how I would meet them. Paul joined a group of tentmakers to get to know people and be part of a community, but what would I do to find a way to be part of this city-centre community I was joining, with opportunities to share the good news of Jesus?

Then there was the issue of money. While having three years' funding from the diocese was amazing, it wouldn't cover all our costs and would pass very quickly. My first incumbency had only been a three-year posting, so I knew from experience what a very short time it is. Over the years I have watched numerous church initiatives burn brightly with initial funding, then quickly burn out once the money has gone. I also knew from being a vicar that there are not great pots of money sloshing around to fund projects like St Clare's. We had already received such generosity from the diocese. We didn't want to assume there would be more money from them, and we didn't want to need it. We wanted to turn that initial generosity into long-term sustainability, hoping that in time we could be as generous to others as they had been to us.

Talking about money was front and centre for all the churches we visited on our sabbatical (except St Paul's, part of Trinity Church Wall Street, which several people joked had more money than God!), and fundraising was a core part of what they did. I met with friends who ran a church they had planted a few years earlier and that had a strong emphasis on social action. They talked me through the numerous and endless funding applications they had to submit in order to keep going.

I was horrified. Getting the grant from the diocese had taken every shred of emotional energy we had, and I never wanted to go through that again. I find fundraising soul destroying, especially looking for grant funding. I was also aware that very few places support core funding, and as we didn't have the same emphasis on social action that our friends' church did, it was unlikely we could get money even if we tried. If we wanted St Clare's to be a long-term project and not just another flash in the pan initiative, we needed to earn our keep, just as Paul did making tents.

From the moment that Morris suggested the old cathedral gift shop for St Clare's, it was clear what the answer was. We needed to run a shop.

While I was in the sixth form and then at university, I worked in a lot of shops. I had a Saturday job at the local bakery. I spent a summer working at the local garden centre and, though I knew next to nothing about plants and gardening, I didn't let this deter me and soon I was chatting confidently with people about rose varieties. I spent another summer in the newsagent's, staffing the till, chatting to regulars, keeping the shelves topped up with stock and looking very disapprovingly at men coming in to buy 'special' magazines, kept behind the counter for them in brown paper bags. After graduating, I spent the first part of a gap year working in Culpeper the Herbalist, a shop that is sadly no more. Here I learned all about essential oils and aromatherapy (slightly frowned upon by my conservative evangelical friends). Naomi's dad owned and ran an independent bookshop and she had spent many hours helping him out.

Between us, we knew a lot about shops and were excited at the idea of having one of our own. The strange shape of the building meant that we could have a worship space at one end and a shop at the other. I loved both aspects of retail work, the selling things and the chatting to people. It would give me a place to meet people in the heart of the community and would also generate some income. Paul was a tentmaker. I would be a shopkeeper.

We were astounded at how God had called us to do something that used all our life experiences, even those things we had never imagined we would need to draw on in ministry.

St Clare's Shop

If a shop was going to be at the heart of our ministry, we wanted to make sure that it was doing some good, and not just adding to the over-consumption problems of the world.

William Morris said, 'Have nothing in your houses that you do not know to be useful or believe to be beautiful.' We decided to have nothing in our shop that we did not know to be useful or believe to be beautiful *and* ethical.

Meanwhile, Bishop's Council was moving slowly but inextricably towards the agonizing conclusion that Offa House, Coventry Diocese's hugely beloved retreat house, had to close. I say hugely beloved. It certainly was by me. Some of my most precious memories and important life moments happened at Offa House. Set in a village about a 20-minute drive from Coventry, it was a huge former vicarage, towering over the tiny church next door, which had been converted and extended into a retreat house. It had been the spiritual heartbeat of the diocese for many years, but lack of investment, lack of vision and lack of use meant it was no longer financially viable, and hadn't been for some time. Like a grand old lady, she was still beautiful and loved, but age and infirmity meant she could no longer do the job she had in her prime.

Offa House was where I spent my ordination retreats and curates' residentials. For several years I would regularly go there to meet with my spiritual director and it was there, in the chapel, that I practised doing communion prior to being priested. I knew and loved every inch of this rambling old building, and was heartbroken at its closure, even though I knew it was the right decision.

Once the decision had been made, the house needed to be emptied, a job that the Ops team at the diocesan office were tasked with. Most of the diocesan staff worked in a large open-plan office, so Naomi was aware of what they were doing. So far they had ordered a couple of large skips and were also trying to itemize everything of value in the hope of finding new homes for them.

Naomi saw an opportunity and now that we were pioneers

there was no time to be coy. We had to be bold. And so one afternoon, when Naomi knew the Ops team would be there, we drove to Offa House, just ten minutes from where we lived, and basically asked if we could look around with a view to taking some stuff.

It was like a treasure trove. We peered into every cupboard in every room, making a long list of all the things we would like. This included the communion table from the chapel, an antique cupboard, a Gopak table, a coffee machine and a lot of crockery, cutlery and other kitchen items.

But as well as things for the church, we also bagged our first stock for the shop. There was a whole cupboard full of beautiful candles that had been sold in their tiny shop. There were hundreds of them. The Ops team were very grateful when we offered to take them. We also stood for a long time in the library, full of thousands of books that had barely been read and were probably destined for the skip, and wondered about what we could do with them.

We submitted our list to the Diocesan Secretary, who was delighted to let us take pretty much everything we wanted. We also asked Richard Cooke, who was in overall charge of clergy and Reader training, about the library. His plan was to take a selection of the books to the diocesan offices, but the rest were ours if we wanted them. We did. And while we were about it, we thought we might as well take the lovely bookcases they were on too. It felt as if even my beloved Offa House was being generous.

Candles and second-hand books were a great start in stocking our new shop, but we needed more than that if we had any chance of reaching sustainability.

When I was about 15, my auntie bought my mum the most exciting Christmas present. It was a word processor. Bear in mind this was in the mid-1980s, so the concept of a word processor was pretty much brand new. I can't remember what make it was, but it comprised a chunky screen, with a slot for a floppy disk, a keyboard and a dot matrix printer. Unlike electric typewriters, you could save your work on the floppy disk and go back and edit it. It was wondrous.

My poor mum was somewhat bemused by it, and so really missed out on a present from her sister-in-law that year. I was entranced and quickly adopted this phenomenal machine as my own. It had a couple of basic programs. One was the word processor, which I used mostly to write essays (it kept me going through O-levels, A-levels and all through university). The other was an incredibly basic desktop publishing program. This I fell in love with. I had always been creative, but my artwork always had a graphic feel to it. I wasn't much good at water-colours or drawing things or the like, but I loved designing posters and could do beautiful calligraphy. Being able to create designs on this exciting new machine was a revelation. I made posters for everything I could think of. The CU programme at school, the church fete, the Christmas sleeping arrangements. I bought brightly coloured paper, and loved watching my pixel-ated designs churn forth noisily from the printer.

It never once occurred to me that maybe I should be a graphic designer. I'm not sure I even knew such a job existed. Instead I remained an enthusiastic amateur, fiercely guarding the job of poster maker at every church I ever went to or led. When I was a very busy vicar, well-meaning people would sometimes try and take the job of poster designer away from me. But I was having none of it. Designing posters and the like has never been work for me, it's just joy. Finally, with our new shop, I could maybe start making some money from this long-held passion.

I set about designing baptism and godparent certificates. At Lillington, we did a lot of baptisms, and it was usually our super-competent parish administrator who filled in all the certificates, including a certificate for each godparent. When, on occasion, it was left to me, it usually ended up with at least one card in the bin. I seemed incapable of remembering that the pink and blue designations of the cards were about the gender of the child, and not the godparent. And so I'd invariably fill in a pink one for a female godparent, before realizing it should have been blue for little Tommy. Aside from the practical issues of making sure you had enough cards of both colours and then remembering how to use them, I also filled them in through gritted teeth, as I railed against the gender stereotyping of children at the very moment of baptizing them into a church which proclaims that in Christ there is no male or female (Galatians 3.28). So I designed baptism and godparent certificates as I had always wanted them. Suitable for all ages, and gender neutral. No messing about with pink and blue or adult and children.

Soon I was designing certificates for all the occasional offices, and then moved on to greetings cards and postcards using artwork that Naomi created as she got better and better at the linocuts.

Lino-cutting isn't Naomi's only creative skill. As long as I have known her she has sewn things. At college it was mostly square-edged things. Curtains, cushion covers and the like. She gradually branched out into more creative things, and while we were at Potters Green made an entire nativity set of child-sized characters using scraps of fabric that the congregation had provided. She occasionally altered or made basic clothes, but never with a pattern, which to her seemed like some strange alchemy.

Then one day a friend suggested that the two of them went on a one-day course to learn how to read a sewing pattern. She agreed, and a few weeks later she disappeared one Saturday morning, clutching the piece of fabric she had bought as instructed. My parents were staying with us for the weekend, and I distinctly remember my mum and I looking at each other in complete astonishment when a few hours later Naomi returned wearing a fabulous, perfectly fitting dress, made from what had left the house as just a piece of fabric. Once she'd learned how to read a pattern there was no stopping her. Soon she was making most of her own clothes, and quite a lot of mine. It didn't stop there, though. She wanted to go further, to be able to design patterns as well. She went on another course, and soon she wasn't just making ordinary clothes, she had created a pattern to make clerical tops. This was a game changer. Women's clericals in our experience were horrible and ill-fitting if you bought them off the peg, or wildly expensive and would take months to come if you had them made to measure. Being able to make them was phenomenal. Surely, we thought, when we opened the shop there would be a market for these? Naomi committed to spending most of her Saturdays sewing clerical tops while I was working in the shop.

But St Clare's is not just a church supplies shop. If the shop was to be our main point of mission and outreach, we wanted anyone walking past to feel that they could come in. So we also sell lots of beautiful gifts, toys and cards. When deciding on what products to stock, we always ask the supplier about their ethical and fair-trade credentials. Recently, we were at a trade show and asked a potential new supplier our usual questions about the people who manufactured their products. The woman's face lit up, as she began telling us by name about the people and families they worked with and got out her phone to show us photos of herself with smiling artisans, creating beautiful products in a spacious workshop. We now sell these gifts.

We had long been inspired by the concept of resource church, the idea that churches who had been given particular input and support from the central church would then resource other churches. As the shop grew, we knew that in our own way, we wanted to be a resource church. We came up with a new strapline for the shop: 'At St Clare's we sell beautiful gifts, innovative and imaginative worship resources and church supplies to help resource our pioneer church community at Coventry Cathedral.'

Over the years, we have tried to see what would be helpful for clergy and churches, and then provide it. People often suggest ideas for things they would love to be able to buy which we then source or create.

Like our baptism sponsor cards. An increasing challenge in parish ministry is parents choosing people to be godparents who aren't themselves baptized, so can't be godparents. Lots of clergy suggest that these people can act as sponsors instead, still committing to pray for and care for the child, but without being official godparents. However, because this is something that has evolved at parish level, and isn't official Church of England policy, there is no provision for them. Wouldn't it be lovely if there was a certificate for them too? So I designed one, making sure it matched the godparent ones.

Many years ago, CMS (the Church Missionary Society) produced a pack called 'The Christ we Share', containing lots of images of Jesus from different cultures. It was hugely radical and was the first time that many of us had seen Jesus portrayed as black or Asian, and even as a woman. This pack went out of print years ago, and I fiercely guarded my pack, only reluctantly lending it out to the many people who kept asking to borrow it. There was clearly a need, so the answer, I decided, was to create a new pack. And so I spent a year hunting for images of Jesus from across the world and through the ages. I must have looked at hundreds, but eventually chose just 40 pictures for our new pack, 'Face to Face with Jesus', including two images created by members of the St Clare's community. Our instinct that there was a need for such a pack was proved right, and it has been one of our bestsellers.

We also love seeking out objects that were never intended for ecclesiastical purposes, but really should have been. We were at a trade show when we spotted some large metal jewellery trees. I'm not sure I know anyone with space in their bedroom for such a thing, but we immediately saw that they would make brilliant prayer trees. Another supplier was selling beautiful wooden cupped hands, marketed as something you might put sweets or business cards in. We sell them as a beautiful worship resource.

We have now even reached the point where we can commission items from some of our suppliers, including a nativity set from Kenya, with black characters (something that is incredibly hard to source), and fairly traded communion sets from India, Mexico and Indonesia.

When we first came up with the idea of St Clare's, the Bishop challenged us to think about how we would grow. Growth for us hasn't been about an ever-bigger church, or planting copies of St Clare's. For us it has become about the sharing of ideas that can enable other churches to flourish and grow: resources that we sell in the shop, ideas for worship freely shared on our website, and happily talking to anyone who will listen about what we do as a church and why.

Every day's a school day

Naomi's clerical tops proved to be so popular that selling them became something of a problem. For the first couple of batches, I put pictures of them on our Facebook page, along with a phone number for people to ring to purchase them. This did not work brilliantly well.

I looked more closely at our website and discovered that there was a way you could add a payment button, so that people could give you money. Sounds so obvious, I know, but bear in mind that we had no website designer, and no training. I had simply been working it out as I went along, enormously grateful that the software had come on enough that I could manage to do that, having tried and failed in the same attempt when at Lillington. I created a 'shop' page, and when the next batch of clerical tops were ready I excitedly added them to the page, and announced their presence on Facebook.

Then followed a completely chaotic hour or so, as I desperately tried to keep track of what had sold and made sure I had removed it from the website before anyone else also paid for it. The payment button wasn't designed for shopping, so had to be removed after each sale. It was carnage. We could usually expect to sell a batch of ten or so tops in less than half an hour. I spent a lot of time apologizing to people and refunding money to people who had bought a top that was already sold.

I cannot really describe the steepness of the learning curve I was on with our website at this point, but with Naomi's help in grasping the basic concept of 'plug ins', I finally understood that I could buy additional software to add to the website which would then enable us to have a proper online shop. The prospect of this was both exhilarating and terrifying. I finally took the plunge in summer 2019 and downloaded the software. I then spent ten minutes looking at it, panicked and decided to ignore it. Well, mostly. Every few weeks, at a quiet moment in the shop, I would open it up and have another look, trying not to panic. And slowly, bit by bit, I began to understand what I was looking at, and how it worked.

In November 2019, we finally had a small online shop ready

to launch. The plan was to use it to sell the clerical tops and a few other bits and pieces such as our baptism and godparent certificates. We set up a new Facebook page to go with it. When the next batch of clerical tops were ready, we put them on the page and announced to the world – well, our Facebook group – that this was where they could be purchased. It was brilliant. However many people there were scrabbling to buy each top, the software dealt with it all, and I just had to offer soothing 'better luck next time' commiserations to those who had failed in their attempt to buy one.

Silver linings

As we entered 2020, we were feeling hugely positive. Things in both the shop and the community were going really well. Like everyone else, we listened with small concern to the slowly emerging news of a nasty sounding new virus in China, but really had no idea of what lay ahead.

We were too busy preparing for the Christian Resources Exhibition, which was to take place in February, at an exhibition centre just ten minutes down the road from us. They had decided to showcase clerical wear with a clergy catwalk and were very keen that, as a local 'company', our wares should be on show. After much negotiation it was agreed that we would take part in the catwalk and have a stand at the show for a fraction of the usual cost. Naomi spent every spare minute sewing, so that we had plenty of tops and dresses to showcase on the catwalk, and then to sell.

Meanwhile, I was making sure that we had other things to sell on the stall, and, with the help of various members of the community, spent hours counting and packaging certificates and cards, and ordering lots of our bestselling products. I added more things to the online shop and printed a flier advertising it. By the time the show arrived, the online shop had gone from being a somewhat pragmatic way to sell clerical tops to a fully fledged church supplies outlet.

Little did we know that this would prove vital to our survival in the months ahead. When the country was plunged into lockdown in March 2020, our first thought was for the well-being of the community, and working out how we could continue to worship and to support one another.

Our second thought was for our finances. Our whole funding model relied on retail and our bricks and mortar shop was closed, probably for months.

I cannot describe how grateful we were to already have an online shop up and running. Most days in early lockdown, I and Dolly the schnauzer would walk into the city centre, where I would spend a couple of hours in the locked shop, painstakingly adding products to the online shop. This was so boring that I think only a national lockdown could have compelled me to do it.

We then started thinking about what resources might be useful to clergy in a pandemic. We produced special cards for churches to send to people, and as Lent approached Naomi came up with the brilliant idea of 'A retreat in a bag'. Lots of clergy go on retreat during Lent, and with all the retreat houses closed, the bag provided an alternative. They really did sell like hot cakes! By now, I was on first name terms with the chaps at the local Post Office.

At the end of 2020, despite the bricks and mortar shop having been closed for nearly half the year, our turnover was significantly higher than in 2019. Our online shop now accounts for nearly half of all our sales. Out of the horror of the pandemic, God managed, as so often happens, to bring some good. Thank God for silver linings.

Dark clouds

We know how fortunate we have been to have received such generosity, but this does not mean that we haven't faced serious challenges.

From the very outset of St Clare's, we were always thinking about the long term and how we could make sure we kept going beyond the initial funding period. We had a clear aim to get to financial sustainability, hopefully by five years in, and in the meantime planned to use the reserves we had built up to plug the gap.

We would also need new licences, as ours ran out at the same time as the funding. To be a working clergy person in the Church of England, you must have a licence. If you are a vicar, then this is relatively straightforward. But as soon as you try and do anything different or pioneering, it quickly becomes almost impossibly complicated.

Two years after we launched, it was time to start talking to the diocese about the future. That meant a conversation with a new archdeacon, as Morris had moved on soon after St Clare's was up and running.

Things went wrong almost immediately. I spoke to the Archdeacon's PA who arranged for an initial meeting with me and the new archdeacon, a first step in the review process. I was surprised that it wasn't me and Naomi but thought it probably didn't matter at this stage. I suggested that rather than me walk over to the diocesan office (which is right next door to the cathedral), maybe he could come to St Clare's so that he could see it, which would help him understand what we were all about.

At the appointed hour, there was no sign of him. Eventually, I phoned his PA to discover that he was in his office waiting for me, having forgotten that he was supposed to be coming to St Clare's. By the time he arrived, we had just 45 minutes. I had already filled in extensive paperwork about our reach and what we were doing, so assuming he had read this I didn't worry too much when we ended up talking mostly about the shop and not a lot about the community. I did, however, feel slightly unsettled when he left. I wasn't at all sure he'd really understood what we were all about.

A couple of weeks later I received a write-up of the meeting. I'd been right to feel unsettled. It seemed I'd somehow failed to communicate the partnership nature of the project, or that we were first and foremost a church community, not a shop. I tried not to worry and waited to hear about the full review process in which Naomi and I together as co-leaders could challenge some of the assumptions and explain again that this was a partnership project between the diocese and the Cathedral, and was, we thought, going rather well.

I was, however, disappointed that he wasn't more interested or more excited about St Clare's. As the diocese was beginning to develop a strategy to start 150 new worshipping communities, I thought we had a lot to offer in terms of wisdom and experience.

Maybe I should have been more proactive, but that's not who I am, and so I waited. And kept waiting. As autumn approached and we'd still heard nothing, we started to get a bit anxious. I spoke to the Dean, who spoke to the Archdeacon, and then it began to become clear that all was not well. It's hard to pin down exactly what happened, as no one was really talking to us, but rather about us, and the hurt of it all clouds memories. But it seemed to me that the Archdeacon had concluded on the basis of one 45-minute conversation that St Clare's should become solely a Cathedral project, with no further input from the diocese. We had no idea what that really meant.

Christmas was coming, so we had no time to really think about it until the new year. Then the world was plunged into a global pandemic. Everything ground to a halt, but pandemic or no pandemic, our licences would soon run out. We needed a plan.

In April 2020, nearly a year after my initial and only conversation with the Archdeacon, we wrote to him outlining our concerns and asking for an opportunity to talk about what was happening next. There was still no response, and so the Dean suggested that we ask for an extension of our licences for a year, giving us time to come up with a proper plan. He put this to the Archdeacon, who then wrote a paper about St Clare's for Bishop's Council, requesting the extension. He hadn't consulted us before writing the paper, which contained inaccurate financial information and made it sound as if we were requesting more money, which we were not. Meaning to be genuinely helpful, I phoned to tell him that the paper was wrong, but hard as I tried I didn't seem able to explain the problem. To my astonishment, he just presented the paper as it was, thereby misrepresenting us.

We did get the extension and then worked hard to try and find a model for our future. I won't bore you with all the gory details of what happened, but after another whole year of anxiety, miscommunication and uncertainty, we were told that as we couldn't *prove* our long-term sustainability I couldn't have a permanent licence as a stipendiary priest, and my current interim licence couldn't be further extended. So we came up with a new plan. I offered to work for minimum wage in the shop, paid from the profits, and then have a licence as a house-for-duty priest.[5] We would continue to live in a church house but without me receiving a stipend. The giving from the St Clare's community would comfortably cover the cost of this. We felt a huge sense of relief at having made this decision, and started to make financial plans accordingly, but to our horror we were then told, by two different people, two different reasons why we couldn't do this.

I began to unravel.

At this point the Cathedral stepped in. The Dean and the Cathedral Chapter were hugely supportive and wanted to find a way that I could continue as a stipendiary minister. They also generously offered to cover our financial shortfall for three years, as we continued to work towards sustainability, so we wouldn't need to use up all our reserves. The relief was massive but short lived as then, seemingly out of nowhere, we heard that because of this, the diocese had decided to withdraw our right to clergy housing.

They 'graciously' said that we could stay in our house but would now need to pay commercial rent, rather than the general clergy housing rate. It was twice as much money for St Clare's to find. Naomi spent pretty much every Saturday of 2019 and 2020 sewing clerical tops to sell in the shop, without taking any money for it, bringing in about the same amount as the increase. This sacrifice of her time, skill and effort would simply be going to pay rent to the diocese for a house that until a moment ago we had been entitled to live in for half the price.

---

5 A 'house-for-duty' job is when a priest appointed to a parish is not paid but is given a house to live in.

A house that had been bought specially for us and St Clare's. We were completely devastated. At that point we had lived in church housing for 22 years. It felt as if the church had broken a covenant with us. It was the final straw. I unravelled in a way that I hadn't since theological college.

I talked to everyone I could. To the Bishop, the Chair of the House of Clergy, the Area Dean, the other archdeacon, the Chief Finance Officer at the diocese ... everyone except the Arch-deacon who had, we assumed, made the decision. I had still only ever spoken to him twice (at that first meeting in 2019, which I was later told was 'the review', and then on the phone prior to the Bishop's Council meeting in May 2020), and Naomi not at all. Eventually we knew there was nothing for it. Staying in the house and paying rent would emotionally and financially destroy us and we didn't trust that in six months' time we might not just be served notice. Naomi was determined. We were going to buy a house, and we were going to do it within eight weeks, so that we would be out of our current house before paying a penny of rent for it.

Through all of this, one thing never changed. Our absolute commitment and sense of calling to St Clare's. Without it, we'd have probably just walked away. I could have found another job, and in fact several well-meaning friends suggested posts that they thought I'd be great at. Naomi, by now, was working in Birmingham and her life could have been a great deal easier if we'd moved diocese.

Reflecting back on it, I am more than ever convinced that new worshipping communities, fresh expressions, pioneer churches – whatever you call them – will only survive if they are born out of calling. While there may be all sorts of good and pragmatic reasons for starting a new worshipping community, if those leading it don't have a strong sense of vocation about the project, when the going gets tough, as it inevitably will, it will be very, very hard to keep going.

We did keep going. At our lowest moments, we always seemed to bump into God, ahead of us, knowing we would be there. In the spring of 2021, when everything seemed impossible, we were in the garden when the swifts arrived. The clear blue sky was suddenly full of dancing, shrieking birds, glad to be home for the summer after their long journey north. It was a moment of transcendence and we put our trust in God afresh, somehow knowing that there would be a way forward. On another occasion, I went for a long walk around a local reservoir to try and untangle my thoughts. Physically tired and emotionally exhausted, I sat on a bench and cried out to God. At that moment, the clouds parted and sunlight poured through. It felt like grace.

In September 2021 we moved into our own house in Coventry, thanks to a very large mortgage and some help from family. I went to the doctor, as by now my mental health was in tatters and I was also experiencing the full force of menopause. I got the help I needed and slowly started to heal. Early in 2022, Mabel the Cavapoo, a fluffy bundle of joy, unexpectedly joined us. Dolly the Schnauzer had died during the first lockdown and we had been without a dog since then. Our new home felt properly like a home, and when the spring came, so did the swifts.

Experience matters

When I was in my early 40s, I went on a training course for clergy who had been in ministry a decade or more and still had as much ministry, maybe more, ahead of them. The idea of the course had been Naomi's, in her role as Clergy Ministerial Development Officer at the diocese. She'd observed that there was lots of training for clergy as they started ministry, first as curates, then as they embarked on a first incumbency. Then there were also various courses for those approaching retirement. But there was nothing specifically tailored for those clergy who had a long time between those two stages of ministry, and that included me. And so off I went on the first of these courses, which those of us attending ended up cheerfully calling the mid-life crisis course.

It was fantastic. For a whole week we talked and reflected and prayed about our ministry with others in a similar place to us. There was an extraordinary level of honesty as we shared our successes and failures and how we were feeling about the second half of our lives and ministries. Without that course I'm not sure I'd have had the courage or self-awareness to hear God's call to start St Clare's.

In all the time we have been running St Clare's, neither Naomi nor I have come across anyone else doing something similar who is mid-ministry. Fresh expressions, pioneer churches, new worshipping communities, whatever you want to call them, when they are clergy-led, tend to be the preserve of curates or as a first post of responsibility. This creates a couple of problems.

First, it often means they are time limited. As a curate, I was given the amazing opportunity to lead the church plant that had recently opened on the new housing development in the parish. When I moved on, as curates mostly do, a couple of years later, it left this fledgling church in a perilous position. They were fortunate to have lots of highly capable people in the community, as well as a mother church that was able to provide the ongoing leadership and support needed until eventually, a decade after being planted, it became a parish church with its own vicar.

New churches that are set up in highly challenging areas, or reaching out to very vulnerable people, are much less likely to keep going if the initial leader leaves after just two or three years, especially if that leader is the person who had the initial vision and calling to get things started. In my admittedly limited knowledge observing church plants that have come and gone in Coventry Diocese, they seem to grind to a halt if either the money runs out or the leader moves on.

As mid-ministry pioneers, we knew we were in it for the long haul. Seven years in, we still feel as committed to and called to St Clare's as we were at the outset. It has also hugely renewed and energized me as a priest.

Second, pioneer ministry is one of the most challenging things I have ever done, and it has taken every ounce of wisdom and knowledge that Naomi and I acquired in each of our 16 years of ministry before launching St Clare's. We have also drawn on the many networks we have built up, the social capital we had accumulated, and the resilience of experience. Pioneers are at the coalface of ministry, and yet so often we send the least experienced to do the hardest work. Many of them do an amazing job, and many seasoned clergy are doing extraordinary pioneer ministry within parish contexts, but wouldn't it be great if a few more mid-ministry clergy could be encouraged to give of their wisdom at the forefront of new initiatives.

Wayside chapel

When I was ten, we went on a family holiday to the Yorkshire Dales. There were ten of us in total. Five adults and five children, of which I was the youngest. There was a lot of walking on this holiday. In fact, it was mostly walking. One day we embarked on a walk to the town of Ingleton, about 100 miles away. I'm kidding, I've no idea how far it was, but it felt like an eternity. Unlike other walks we had done, which included climbing and soaring views as well as quite a lot of drizzle, this one was just a trek along a seemingly endless track in uncharacteristic baking hot sunshine. By the time we reached our destination we were hot and tired and fed up. Of course, the bad news was that after a potter around and some lunch, we had to walk back the way we came.

Reflecting on it, the walk home must have been even more miserable for the adults than for the children, as they had to endure our moaning and jolly us along. What kept us going was the promise of an ice cream. At some point on the walk heading out, we had passed a small hut selling drinks and ice creams. We were assured that on our way back, we could have one.

As we trekked back along the endless track, every time we turned a corner, or came over the brow of a hill, we were sure that the ice cream hut would be there. It wasn't. Again and again, when we were absolutely sure we'd reached the point we'd passed it on the way, we were disappointed. Eventually, at the point when we had more or less given up hope, like an oasis in the desert, we spotted it in the distance. We walked on with a new spring in our steps, as we finally made it to a place of rest and refreshment. The rest of the walk home was just that bit easier.

Some of the things about St Clare's we had envisioned, others we had not. We had thought of the shop as a way to make money and as a way to do outreach in the sense of inviting people to join us for worship on a Sunday.

We had not thought about it having a ministry in its own right beyond that. But early on, one of our members described St Clare's as a wayside chapel, a place where people on a spiritual journey could come in and pause a while. We are like that ice cream shop, welcoming weary travellers and offering spiritual rest and refreshment.

We had only been open a few days, when a young woman hurried into the shop, out of the rain, to see if we sold umbrellas. We did. As she paid for it she noticed my clerical collar. She asked if I was a vicar. I said yes. She started to leave, but turned back at the door. She returned to the shop counter and started to tell me her story and about what a dark place she was in. I listened, interrupted from time to time by other customers, and then eventually prayed with her. She thanked me and left saying she felt a lot better.

It's rare for a day to go by when I don't talk and pray with a complete stranger about something that's going on in their life. Sometimes it's people who have walked into the cathedral and just been overwhelmed by the presence of God and don't know how to respond. For others, they've come to buy a cross or a rosary following the death of a loved one, and leave also with a blessing. Some people walk in knowing they want to talk, others just open up when they see my collar. Somehow, despite all the failings of the church and the clergy, a clerical collar still gives people the confidence to know that this is someone they can talk to. Sometimes we just chat at the counter, sometimes we go and sit in the worship area. I have prayed with people of many different faiths and of none. Some return time and again, others I see only once. It is the most extraordinary privilege. Occasionally they come back some time later to say thank you for the spiritual ice cream they received from St Clare's at a moment when they had almost given up hope.

Numerous other people come in and pause and look at the worship space, asking what we do there. Every day I get to tell people about St Clare's, and invite them along. It's how a good number of our community have joined us. When the shop is open, we offer the worship space to be used for free by local charities needing a meeting space.

At times when I am feeling uncertain about St Clare's, when I am tired, or my faith is weak, that is so often the moment when someone walks in and finds a priest, freely available for them to talk to. Sometimes it's a member of the community, sometimes a local clergy person, often it's a complete stranger. Then I know that this is one of the most profound and generous things we do.

St Clare's is situated on St Michael's Avenue, an ancient thoroughfare that runs from the city, through the cathedral and onwards to what is now Coventry University. Hundreds of people walk past each day, from all over the world, as people have walked up and down that road for hundreds of years. Mostly they walk on by, but for some, seeing the sign outside, declaring we are open and inviting them in, can be life changing.

Dave

Dave (not his real name, but the one he chose for this, as a memorial to his friend who died) was one of those people. I don't remember the first time he ventured into the shop, but it was the very early days of St Clare's. I do remember the first proper conversation I had with him, and how much I enjoyed it. Dave is in his 70s and a proper Coventrian, his life shaped by the culture and music of the city where he grew up. So much so that he is always dressed in black and white, with the familiar checkerboard pattern of the two-tone movement, a genre of music that sought to transcend and defuse racial tensions, which originated in Coventry in the late 1970s.

Dave began to pop in from time to time, always soon after I had opened, and in time I learned that this was because he liked to get out and about while it was still quiet. Dave suffers from crippling PTSD. He fought in the Falklands War and saw his best friend killed just yards away from him. This kind of trauma cannot fail to have an impact, but for Dave it didn't really hit him until years later.

He was telling me one day how he wanted to go to an Armed Services Day service at Holy Trinity, a large church just a stone's throw from the cathedral, but wasn't sure if he was up to it. He planned to go in last, and sit at the back, so he could easily leave if the noise and the people became too much.

I sensed a longing for community, and at some point suggested that coming to church at St Clare's might be OK for him, and perhaps he should try it. He was already familiar with the space, and I talked him through how things worked so there would be no surprises.

To my amazement, one Sunday he appeared, and then the following Sunday, and then the one after that, and soon he was a beloved member of our small and new community. He would usually arrive first, and he would always sit in the same chair, the one nearest the door. He would stay and chat for a while after the service, regaling us with extraordinary tales of his time in the army. He was absolutely nothing like the rest of us, but somehow fitted right in.

He didn't often share in the services, but one Sunday in Advent, when I had used the illustration of a telescope in talking about John the Baptist, he spoke. He tentatively talked about how being at St Clare's had enabled him to see God more clearly. How it was like looking through a telescope, and God had been brought near to him. He shared with me how his confidence had grown, and how much more at peace he was. It was a joy to see the gentle hand of God at work in his life.

We began to lose touch with him during the pandemic. He had no interest in joining us via Zoom, even when we offered to show him how. We sent him regular notes and texts, and as life returned to normal he came back a couple of times, but eventually disappeared and it's been a long time since I saw or heard from him.

Little changes that helped St Clare's as a whole did not help Dave, and that grieves my heart. I changed the shop opening time from 10.30 to 11.00 a.m., which meant that he no longer dropped in to see me on his way home from town, as it was too late. The community also grew. Not a lot, but enough to make him feel uncomfortable. The last time I saw him, he said that it just didn't feel like his place any more.

St Clare's is not perfect, far from it, and I often wonder if there was more we could have done (or still could do) to support Dave. Sending him this chapter to read led to a conversation in which he said he might come back, and that made my heart sing. But even if he doesn't, for a season, the open door of St Clare's was a gift to Dave, and he was a gift to us.

Open

'Come to me, all you that are weary and are carrying heavy burdens, and I will give you rest. Take my yoke upon you, and learn from me; for I am gentle and humble in heart, and you will find rest for your souls. For my yoke is easy, and my burden is light.' (Matthew 11.28–30)

Misfits welcome

Some years ago, when Facebook was just beginning to get really popular, like so many others (I assume), I decided to do a bit of light stalking of some of my old school friends, people I had been incredibly close to as a child and young adult but had long since lost touch with. I discovered two things.

First, the girl I had been best friends with at middle school had gone on to have a very successful career as a model. She had been a very pretty child who had grown into a very beautiful woman.

Second, I discovered that the boy I had been best friends with (and desperately in unrequited love with) at high school was gay; now married to a very attractive husband with a couple of lurchers. I'd had no idea.

It was a lightbulb moment. No wonder I had always felt somewhat unattractive. I had no idea that she was an impossible comparison and that he was never going to reciprocate my feelings. Not their fault. Not my fault. But it all added to a feeling that I didn't quite fit, or wasn't quite good enough. Other things added to this sense of feeling that I was always just slightly on the outside of things.

I remember being in the school car park. I have no idea why. I was chatting to Mr Smith (not his real name; truth be told, I can't remember what he was called). He was a supply teacher, swooping in from time to time to cover physics or maths lessons. He was also a Christian. And on a Tuesday lunchtime, when he was around, he would come along to the school's Christian Union, to offer support and encouragement to us little band of faithful souls who met to chat, to pray and to study our Bibles. I was 15 years old. I had been in the CU for not much over a year, and it had changed my life.

Since arriving at high school aged 13, life there had become increasingly unbearable. I was constantly being bullied, and it was like a slow drip eating away at my soul. Lunchtimes were a living nightmare. I would spend as much time as I could in the library and would sometimes resort to hiding in the toilets. The very pretty best friend had not moved with me from middle school and I was adrift, without a group I really fitted into. I dreaded that long and lonely hour each day, which felt like an eternity.

But then one day, out of nowhere, a miracle happened. I was sitting on a bench in a corridor waiting for the minutes of lunch to tick by when I heard someone call my name. I looked up to see Heidi and Natalie standing in front of me. They were two of the bright and shiny, pretty girls for whom high school seemed so effortless. They were also Christians. But not like I was a Christian. I sang in the choir at the somewhat staid and trad-itional high church in the small town where I grew up, pretty much the only teenager in the place. They went to St Paul's, the exciting evangelical church in the city, where there was a youth group and a band and a trendy vicar.

They spoke to me.

'We're going to CU. Would you like to come?'

Like those first disciples in the Gospels, without a word, without a backward glance, without hesitation, I stood up and followed. I had found a place to belong.

Joining the CU was a gateway to a whole other world. Soon I was also a member of the youth group at St Paul's, and would sometimes go to the evening services there, where we sang songs instead of hymns, and prayed out loud. I also joined a home group that met just a five-minute walk from my house.

So back to the car park and Mr Smith.

The CU needed a new leader. With exams looming, the current one had stepped down. Mr Smith and I were chatting about who it might be. We were all a little bit in awe of Mr Smith. He would entrance us with tales of his exciting missionary endeavours in Mozambique. He was attractive, charismatic and intelligent and treated us like grown-ups. He gave the CU members time and attention that none of the other kids got, and that made us feel so special. As he and I chatted in the car park he talked about who might take over the CU. He said there was someone who showed real potential, who had natural leadership ability, even if they didn't realize it. A warm glow spread through me, as I waited for him to ask me if I would consider taking on the leadership role. I knew I had the skills to do it, but having someone like Mr Smith notice was a huge encouragement to a still very fragile soul.

But then it gradually, horribly dawned on me that he wasn't talking about me. He was talking about Heidi. Heidi, who had said she had no interest in leading the CU. He couldn't see me, because he couldn't see past Heidi. Not her fault. She was, and still is, lovely. But she was ridiculously pretty, with long red hair and sparkling green eyes. She was full of confidence and had an infectious laugh to go with her mischievous sense of humour. She also came from an impeccable evangelical background. Poor Mr Smith. With the benefit of hindsight, I can see that he was very young and she was very appealing. But his bedazzlement was crushing to me. I still remember that awful feeling of rejection settling in the pit of my stomach. In the space of moments, my teenage self had gone from feeling on top of the world, to feeling like a complete failure. All the confidence and joy I had gained in the preceding year was in danger of just draining away as I realized that I still didn't fit.

Fortunately, God is bigger than Mr Smith's fallibility, and there were other people in my life who could see my potential, and so I did end up leading the CU. But that small encounter in a car park still lives with me nearly 40 years later.

Naomi has similar stories to tell of her school years, and when we started St Clare's we really wanted it to be a place where those people who always felt like they didn't quite fit in, who sensed they didn't quite match up to an unspecified standard, who knew what it was to be on the outside, could find a place to really belong. We wanted to be open to them.

No judgement here

Holding to a value of being open also means trying very hard to let people be who they are without judgement.

One Sunday, when I was in my mid-20s, living and working just outside Coventry, my vicar invited me round for a chat. I wasn't sure why, but it wasn't unheard of. I was in the vocations process, so occasional one-to-ones were pretty normal. I lived just a couple of minutes from the vicarage, in a village near where I worked and where I was lodging with an eccentric middle-aged divorcee. Robert was the vicar of the village church, where I had found a lovely and welcoming community. I had also found a boyfriend. More precisely, a man friend. He was 47 years old, divorced and had a son the same age as me. He had recently come to faith, having been invited to church by an old friend. He worked in television and seemed wildly glamorous to me. We had starred together in the church Christmas musical and romance had blossomed. I was initially bowled over, not least by a powerful physical attraction, but quite quickly I began to have doubts about whether it really was such a good idea. I'd make a decision to break it off, but then somehow, when I was with him, couldn't quite go through with it. I'd been really lonely, and a less than perfect relationship was better than being on my own.

The chat with Robert, as it turned out, was about the boyfriend. He too had his doubts about the relationship, and gently suggested that maybe I shouldn't get 'too involved'. His instincts were right and he meant well, but the well-intentioned chat had entirely the opposite effect to that which he had intended.

Like most people, my personality has contradictory traits. I don't like to stand out too much, and value conformity (I always worry about whether I am over- or under-dressed for social occasions) and instinctively want to fit in, follow the rules and not get into any trouble. But I also hate being told what to do. And in particular, as someone who is so at pains to be a responsible, rules-following kind of person, having my behaviour questioned, however reasonably, really, really irks me. So Robert telling me I should think about ending my relationship did not go down well. Instead of listening to his wisdom (he was absolutely right), I dug my heels in, and it now became impossible for me to end the relationship since it would look as if I'd done it because he told me to, and he'd be all pastoral and lovely about it while actually thinking, 'I told you so!'

I was very young and naïve, so I spurned the advice and got myself way too deep into a relationship that would inevitably end in a horrible mess and heartbreak; but it took four years. The four years weren't all bad. There was a huge amount I loved about him and we had some wonderful times. But we also hurt each other a great deal. I hurt him through my naïve belief that I could fix him and learn to live with him despite my reservations. Not ending it sooner was cruel, when I knew deep down that I would eventually leave him. He hurt me, as I was simply too young to cope with the enormity of his emotional baggage and increasingly serious mental health issues. I became more and more afraid that if I did leave him, his life would implode and disaster would follow. And sadly, I was right. A few years later, after a slow downward spiral, he ended up in prison. I was left with an enormous amount of guilt to deal with, as well as berating myself for giving four years of my 20s to a person whom I knew I didn't love enough to spend my life with.

I am not blaming Robert for any of this (he was an excellent vicar). Things might have turned out exactly the same even without 'the chat'. But it certainly didn't help.

What it has done has really helped inform my approach to pastoral care (not without making some dreadful mistakes along the way). Over the years, I have become increasingly open in my approach. If people want to talk to me (whether at their invitation or mine) I try really hard to listen, and to accept them exactly as they are. This seems even more important now

I'm ministering to young people, whose lives are full of change and challenge and seemingly endless decisions.

It seems that my role as a priest and pastor is to help them develop the tools to make good decisions as followers of Jesus, as well as the tools to know what to do when things don't turn out as they hoped, or things just go wrong. I want them to know Jesus; to know his teaching and values; to know that he loves them no matter what; to know that mess-ups can be forgiven; and to know the voice of the Holy Spirit guiding and upholding them. I want them to be able to discern for themselves what is right and have the courage to act on it. I don't want them to need me to tell them what they should do, and I don't want to pass judgement, as no situation can really be understood from the outside. I will give advice if asked, but I try very hard to wait until I am asked. The times when I haven't, it has usually gone really badly, and I'm not sure anyone ever took any unsolicited advice I offered anyway. Of course there are exceptions, but the times when someone has been doing something so heinous that I've felt compelled to step in have been mercifully few.

And so I try to be as open as I can with people, accepting them just as they are, however they identify, whatever their relationship status, however they are choosing to live their life. And if things in their life need to change, it's God's job to sort that out, not mine.

Seeing is believing

On 24 April 1994, I and my friend Lucy (a school friend visiting for the weekend) sat on the Queen's steps at Coventry Cathedral and watched the ordination of the first women priests in the cathedral. We watched through the great glass west screen – there was no room inside! One of those new priests was the curate at my village church. On the following Sunday I watched her preside at communion and, finally, the scales fell off and my eyes were opened. Three weeks later I started on my journey to ordination.

For years, people had been asking if it was something I had thought about, but somehow I just never heard them. It took me seeing a woman priest in action to hear it. I am so immensely grateful to those women who had more imagination than I did; who could hear God calling them to a ministry that they weren't yet allowed to do; to a ministry they had never seen a woman doing. Not all of us are capable of that, which is why representation is so important. Some of us need to see someone like us doing a thing, in order to realize we too can do it.

And it's not just about the big things, or even doing things at all. Seeing other people like you in any context makes belonging so much easier. One Sunday at St Clare's, we were talking about how God might use all aspects of who we are in his service. Joanne, who is deaf, said that her very presence as a disabled person was something God could use. Other disabled people coming to church would know that they were welcome and valued and not alone.

Sadly, there have been many moments in my life when I have felt as if I didn't quite belong in church, or that something about me needed to change to really fit in, even with all my white middle-class privilege. But that moment of seeing Liz standing behind the communion table proclaiming 'The Lord is here' is one I hold onto as we seek to ensure that our community is as diverse as possible, so that anyone walking in might just spot someone a bit like them, and think, 'Yes, it's OK for me to be here.'

What do you mean I can't be a bishop?

Sometimes, exclusion is structural, and however open and welcoming we are, until the structures change, there will be people to whom we just cannot be fully open.

I have a confession. When I was starting training for ordination I hadn't realized that women couldn't be bishops; that I couldn't be a bishop. I must have just assumed that when women were allowed to be priests, that included bishops. I only properly engaged with the subject when General Synod began to talk about it. To be clear, I did not have, and never have had, any inclination to be a bishop, but I was outraged to discover that the door was closed to me, even if it wasn't a door I had any desire to open. There's a white-hot rage that boils up inside me when I am told I can't do something without good reason. If I'm prepared to put in the time and effort to acquire the necessary skills and experience, then why can't I do it? Or at least be considered? Old boys' clubs, appointments without due process, lists of special people, these things all make me mad, really mad.

And so I started paying attention. And on that fateful day in November 2012, I sat with my ear glued to my computer (it was before the days of video streaming), listening to every word of the long and increasingly rancorous debate leading up to that first vote to decide if women could be bishops in the Church of England. It needed a two-thirds majority in each of the three Houses (laity, clergy and bishops) to pass. It didn't. The laity voted it down. I was stunned. Then I was upset. Then I was angry. Really angry.

The injustice of being denied the possibility of a job that I do not want, just because of my gender, may seem a small thing compared to the truly appalling, life-limiting injustices that women in Afghanistan, Iran and sadly so many other places in the world still face. But my rage was part of their rage. If we can't even manage to dismantle the patriarchy here, in the Church of England, then what hope is there for women in places where they are denied even an education?

I didn't know what to do with my anger. Then just a few weeks later one of our General Synod reps got a job as an archdeacon in another diocese, and so a new clergy member needed electing. It seemed clear that, if I didn't like what General Synod were doing, then I should stand for election. There were six candidates: me, and five men. I won by a landslide.

I was fortunate. God gave me a way to channel my anger to effect change. Not everyone gets that chance. Just two years later I was there, part of the Synod that voted to allow women bishops, one of the greatest privileges of my life.

However, it was at a price, allowing those who disagreed

with the legislation to opt out of accepting the authority of a female bishop. They would instead have a specially appointed male bishop who shared their views. There is no time limit on this arrangement and new priests continue to be ordained who do not recognize women priests or bishops. I am not OK with this, even though I voted for it. In hindsight I think it was a mistake, and ten years later feels something like being in debt to a loan shark, demanding a seemingly eternal and increasingly hard to bear return on their credit.

The experience of exclusion, however small, seems to me entirely contrary to the gospel, and I don't understand why churches seem time and again to put up barriers to entry, when we should surely be flinging wide the gates. I wanted to belong to, and to lead, a church where when we said, 'All are welcome', we really meant it.

One chair does not fit all

Other times, it's the physical infrastructure that excludes people and prevents us being open to all. And that's not always as obvious as ramps and hearing loops.

During our sabbatical, prior to starting St Clare's, we attended an event with a friend who is considerably heavier than average. We were having a lovely day, but had been on our feet a lot and were all in need of a cup of tea, and probably a piece of cake as well. We made our way to the café and were grateful to see that it wasn't too busy. We set about choosing a table. Then suddenly, inexplicably, our friend said that he'd changed his mind, that he didn't want a cup of tea after all, and had just remembered he was meeting up with some other friends. Or something like that. After making what were clearly excuses for something, he speedily disappeared.

As Naomi and I sat down (slightly gingerly as the chairs were not the most robust, and neither of us is exactly slim!), it dawned on us that this was why our friend had scarpered. It was the chairs. Not only were they a bit flimsy looking, but they were not very wide, with narrow arms. Our friend just wouldn't fit in them. Until that moment I had never given chairs much thought. At least not in that way. I had thought about whether a chair (especially a church chair) was comfy or not, and have sat in some almost intolerably uncomfortable pews, but I had never had to worry about whether I would physically fit in a chair, or if it would take my weight.

We had been pondering on what kind of chairs to put in St Clare's, and it now became clear that what we chose said as much about our openness, and whether we were genuinely inclusive, as any welcoming words. We were horrified at the thought of someone walking in and feeling panicked and humiliated by the seating.

Nice modern church chairs are pretty good, but we didn't have the budget for them, and they didn't really fit the vibe we were going for in what would become our worship space. Once again, it was Naomi's creative thinking that gave us the answer. Lloyd Loom chairs. Those wonderful woven chairs, made of paper no less, that can be found lurking in the corner of every antique shop in the country, chairs on which many of our mothers or grandmothers will have nursed their babies, chairs that sometimes turn out to be beautifully disguised commodes, chairs made for every purpose for 150 years, and which are still manufactured today.

We set about scouring every antique shop in the area for these lovely old chairs. We asked friends. We looked on eBay. We tried not to spend more than £40 on a chair, got some for as little as a fiver and some for free. This strange assortment of chairs, of varying colours, styles and conditions, gathered in our garage. There were chairs suitable for tall people and short people, skinny people and wider people, people with bad backs, people who struggled to get up, and those who just wanted something really cosy and comfy to sink into.

Once we had collected about 20 chairs, Naomi took them all into the garden and embarked on the labour of love needed to transform them from scruffy, ill-matching chairs to a symbol of welcome and comfort. She spray-painted them all in various shades of teal, to match the decor in the space, and re-upholstered all the ones that had cushions. When she had finished, they looked amazing. Each one different, but clearly matching. Just like us; all human, but each of us unique, and with our own seating needs and preferences.

One of our members, who has a disability, was away one Sunday as she was visiting her parents and went to their church, the church she grew up in. When she returned, she told us of the startling revelation she had made. She had always thought she just didn't like the worship style there but in fact, it was the uncomfortable chairs that were the problem, and the expectation that you would sit on them. At St Clare's there are a choice of chairs, and if she wants to, she is also welcome to sit on the rugs on the floor, which people often do.

Open-minded

There is a story in Mark's Gospel (Mark 7.24–30) where Jesus encounters a Gentile woman of Syrophoenician origin. She has a child who is desperately ill and begs Jesus to heal her. Jesus seems to be outrageously rude to her, and many people reasonably struggle with this story because of that. He compares Gentiles to dogs and tells her to go away. But she is having none of it. Her child is ill and she refuses to give up. Instead, she stands up to Jesus and demands that he takes her seriously. Her words change his mind, and her daughter is healed. It blows my mind every time I read it. If even Jesus can change his mind, then who am I to think that I have all the answers about pretty much anything? Being open means being open-minded, being willing to hear other points of view, to talk about them, and to be prepared even to change your mind.

I have listened to the *Today* programme on Radio 4 every morning for as long as I can remember. Most days, then, I have also listened to a 'Thought for the Day'. But of all the hundreds (thousands?) of thoughts I must have heard, there is really only one that has stayed with me.

It was at some point in the mid-1990s and was given by Anne Atkins. She was talking about homosexuality (I'm not sure why) and in summary said that we should hate the sin but love the sinner. She was very clear: same-sex relationships were wrong. I was very clear: I disagreed with her.

This presented me with a problem. I was in my mid-20s and had spent my life trying really hard to fit in. And since joining the CU at school, the place I had tried hardest to fit in was at church. More precisely, the charismatic evangelical Anglican churches that had become home.

I think that deep down I knew that I didn't agree with quite a lot of the teaching I heard, but didn't dare say so out loud. Surely it must be me who is wrong? I had no idea that eventually this tension I was living with would pull me apart. I had no idea then that there were huge rafts of the church with very different views on issues such as homosexuality. I had grown up in the central tradition of the Anglican Church but we never talked about these things, so I didn't even know what they thought on the matter.

Listening to Anne Atkins, I was surprised by the strength of my reaction. I couldn't stop thinking about it. I was desperate to talk to someone about how I was feeling, but who? Friends who weren't Christians would think I was being ridiculous and friends who were would no doubt start praying for the well-being of my mortal soul, as a liberal backslider.

And so I kept quiet. Very quiet. I was scared that if I stood up and said what I thought, I would be ejected from the fold, and the thought of that was simply unbearable. But it was on that morning, listening to Anne Atkins, that I realized this wasn't a sustainable position. I'd love to say that I immediately did something about it. I did not. It took me years, and an unravelling at theological college, to finally accept that what I believed was OK.

It is hard to explain the power of the pulpit for some young people who are eager to serve God and to be welcomed into the church fold. It took me a long time even to acknowledge that someone who preached standing in such an exalted position could be wrong, let alone that I could express that out loud. This may sound ridiculous to some, but I know I'm not alone in this. For me, as a now very seasoned preacher and teacher, it has meant that I am always cautious with my words (maybe too much so), so eager am I for no one to feel they can't disagree with me.

Spiritual conformity

Being open also means acknowledging that all of us will meet with God in our own way, and no one way is better than another. Spiritual conformity is not only unnecessary, but potentially harmful.

The church I joined as a teenager had been hugely influenced by the charismatic revival of the 1970s and '80s. I didn't really understand what this meant at the time, but came to learn that as a proper Christian I could expect regularly to be filled with the Holy Spirit, in an unmistakable way that would result in me speaking in tongues and possibly falling over, and maybe also have other gifts of the Spirit such as words of knowledge or interpretation of tongues. I quickly got the sense that if I didn't experience this there was something wrong with me, that somehow I was resisting God's work in my life. I attended a home group, and in time agreed to be baptized with the Holy Spirit. Everyone seemed more excited about this than me, but I loved how much they loved and welcomed me. I wanted to fit in, so I let them pray for me. They surrounded me, laying on hands and praying both in English and in tongues. I opened my heart, expectantly waiting for the Spirit to do something. Time passed. They prayed more fervently. But nothing happened. I just felt vaguely deflated, and then disappointed, and then guilty, as I had to bear the weight of everyone else's disappointment too.

The leaders reassured me that it wasn't a problem, God worked in different people in different ways, and that sometimes it took time for the Spirit to manifest itself. I took heart and assumed that I just needed to be patient. But somehow, in all the time I was part of the charismatic church, I never quite experienced what everyone else seemed to be experiencing. I discovered that I could speak in tongues, but was never convinced that it had anything much to do with the Holy Spirit. I attended huge charismatic events including one led by the very influential John Wimber. I distinctly remember being in a large church full of people singing and swaying and falling over, apparently entirely taken over by the Spirit, and feeling like the odd one out. Was it me, or was it them?

I did have profound moments of encounter with God, but never in the way that seemed expected. They were usually (and continue to be) as a response to something I was struggling with, and manifested as a deep sense of something in my inner being. No easy answers, but a clarity of thought and purpose. Over the years I learned to understand that God communicates with us in so many different ways, and that the Spirit is a part of my very being, not an outward force compelling me to think or feel or do things. But I had to learn that lesson for myself, as no one in the church seemed able to understand when I tried to explain, and mostly just seemed sorry for me! On the whole it was mildly frustrating as it added to my sense of not quite belonging, but didn't dim my enthusiasm for God or the church. On a few occasions, however, something would happen, or more likely not happen, that would cause me deep distress, and rather than the church nurturing my delicate teenage sense of self-worth, it acted to diminish it.

I remember one such occasion when some of us from the youth group had planned to go to an event (I forget what or where). Lifts were arranged, but somehow there had been a mix-up and no one arrived to pick me up. I was upset, but I resolved that it would all be OK, I just needed to pray about it. I had been reading *Anything You Ask* by Colin Urquhart, and he assured me that if I prayed with enough faith, commitment and specificity (don't just pray for a bicycle, but pray for a red bicycle if that is what you want), then God would grant my request. I wanted nothing as audacious as a bike, just that someone would notice I was missing and come and collect me and take me to a worthy Christian event. No problem. I prayed. I waited. I prayed harder. I waited some more. No one came. I got really upset. Mum found me crying and I told her what had happened (about the lift mix-up, that is, not the praying) and she tried to reassure me and asked if it was too late to phone someone to see what was happening. I have no recollection of

how this tale of woe ended, but it definitely wasn't with someone turning up at my door having been prompted by the Spirit
to come and fetch me. I think my lovely mum probably gave
me a lift.

Open to doubt

I arrived at theological college in September 1997, excited for
all it would bring, but also apprehensive. I had been in a relationship with the aforementioned boyfriend for four years, but
deep down I knew he wasn't my for ever person, but didn't
know quite how to get out of it. And so, just before I headed
off to St John's, I did what anyone battling deep uncertainties
about a relationship should do – I agreed to marry him! And so
I headed off to college with a ring on my finger. Quite soon after
starting college, I began to get panic attacks, a new and awful
experience for me. To start with I couldn't grasp quite why I
was now so distressed, when on the face of things everything in
my life was so good. Some of my new college friends dragged
me off wedding-dress shopping, and as I stood and looked at
myself in the mirror, in a beautiful ivory gown, I finally knew I
really had to end it.

Breaking up was every bit as awful as I had imagined it would
be. As his life unravelled, I had to accept the wisdom of those
around me. He wasn't my responsibility, it wasn't my fault,
and I didn't owe him anything. But the panic attacks didn't
stop. My thirtieth birthday was looming, and the reality of
everything I had given up to be at college hit me.

Then, worst of all, I would wake up in the middle of the night
with this terrible thought. What if God doesn't exist? What if
all this was for nothing? Looking back, it was as if my whole
theological framework and understanding was unravelling, like
a hand-knitted jumper. Soon I had nothing but a tangled pile
of wool.

From the moment I had first arrived at the exciting charismatic evangelical church as a teenager thirsty for connection
and for God, I had had reservations about the theology, the

style of worship and whether I really belonged there. I don't think I could have even begun to express or understand that at the time, I was just so desperate to fit in, to be part of the in crowd. And there was so much I loved about it. I am incredibly grateful for the friends I made, the love people showed me, and the tremendous grounding in the Bible I received. But the reality was that long before I arrived at St John's, deep-seated questions were beginning to emerge. So deep that I began to doubt that God even existed.

I am so grateful that in the midst of this there were people who allowed me to ask even the most challenging of questions, who didn't judge me, tell me that I was wrong, or what I ought to think. They kept the faith for me, when it seemed like I had none. This included Naomi.

I met her on the first day of theological college. She was just 22 years old. I was 27 and she apparently thought I was very grown-up and wise. We hit it off immediately. There was a definite chemistry between us, and a glorious ease of conversation. We were both living in a small block of self-contained bedsits available for single students at the college who needed year-round accommodation. I was on the ground floor and she on the third floor.

I was initially nervous about the strength of our connection. Having just disentangled myself from one all-consuming relationship, I was worried about charging headlong into another. I didn't want to end up dependent on just one person again.

Unlike me, Naomi had no doubts about her faith, and that was such a gift. She never judged me for my uncertainties, but instead had enough faith for both of us. It was Naomi who was there for me when I got back to college having broken off my engagement. It was Naomi who was there when I couldn't stop shaking with the panic attacks. And it was Naomi who was there as we grappled with new theology, wrote essays and preached our first sermons. By the end of three wonderful years at St John's, having supported one another through heartbreaks and challenges, and rejoiced together in our moments of success and inspiration, it was clear that we would spend our lives together (probably a bit clearer to Naomi, but she always sees things before me and has just that bit more vision and certainty than I do).

I was blessed to have three years full time at college, and after unravelling in year one I spent the next two years slowly and carefully knitting myself a new theological jumper. Many of the evangelical 'truths' I had been taught didn't make it into the new jumper. Nor did certainty. I learned to live with doubt, facing it rather than hiding from it. I realized that the Christian life had to be about more than personal salvation and being sure of my place in heaven. It had to make a difference now. It had to make the world a better place now. If God didn't exist, then I wanted to be sure that the life I chose to live, serving God as a priest, was still the right one. My ministry had to be one that gave people hope, purpose and community, that helped them flourish.

When we started St Clare's, we knew it had to be OK for people to be there even if they were riddled with doubts, or didn't really know what, if anything, they believed. If we were a community that people felt able to be part of, despite their uncertainties, then that would be success.

Finally open

We finally opened for worship on 16 September 2017. The first Sunday was terrifying. We had no idea who, if anyone, would turn up. Would we be sitting there on our own, wondering what on earth had made us think this was a good idea?

To our amazement, seven people showed up.

The extraordinary thing was that right from that very first Sunday, the people who came were exactly the people we had been longing and praying would come.

We have welcomed people who, for all sorts of reasons, had just drifted away from church. We have welcomed people who had left churches because they could no longer stay in a place with very conservative teaching. At least one person was excluded from the church they had been a faithful and active member of for many years. We have welcomed people who are just taking their first tentative steps towards Jesus. We have welcomed students from the universities. We have welcomed people who have moved to Coventry and sought out an inclusive church to be part of. We have welcomed people whose lives were at rock bottom and just needed a place to belong. Some have found their way to us through word of mouth. Some have come across our website. Some walked past the building and read our vision statement. Others came into the shop and I invited them to join us.

Of the seven who came on week one, five of them came back and soon became the core of our fragile little new community.

Every week for the first year, maybe more, we braced ourselves for the possibility that this might be the week when no one other than us showed up. So far, that has never happened. In fact, except for just one week, there have never been fewer than six of us.

Proud to be woke

One morning, I was in St Clare's, talking to a clergy friend who comes in for a chat over a coffee every so often, when a tall, white, older man came into the shop and spent a bit of time looking at the books. He then walked over to us, and without preamble decreed that these days he had atheistic leanings, because he was tired of the church and the way it was going. I sighed inwardly, it's sadly something I've heard before. People leaving the church because they can no longer cope with attitudes that seem to exclude rather than welcome people, that judge people rather than loving them.

'Oh, I'm sorry to hear that ...', I ventured, before the man loudly continued.

'Yes, the church these days is just too "woke". I mean, what's this nonsense about using the word "humankind" when "mankind" is a perfectly good word, and everyone knows that man means all people ...?'

He had more to say, but you get the general gist.

My friend (a white man himself) tried gently to suggest that maybe being 'woke' wasn't about him, and maybe other people found the word 'man', meaning all people, to be difficult. I was simply smiling through gritted teeth, wishing I was wearing a Smash the Patriarchy t-shirt.

Our visitor was having none of it. He laughingly decreed that he liked to be provocative, and if people didn't like him, so be it. I, for one, I'll be honest, did not warm to him. From his place of privilege, I don't think this man had ever stopped to consider whether being provocative wasn't just an intellectual thing for the people he provoked, but actually caused them harm, caused them to feel lesser. He didn't seem remotely interested in how his views might make other people feel.

During the summer of 2022, we had a sermon series called 'Included', where we consciously chose to hear stories about how church has not always been a safe or welcoming place because of other people's views and attitudes. I was so incredibly moved that members of St Clare's courageously shared their stories about neurodiversity, disability, mental health and poverty, just four of a long list of things that can deliberately or inadvertently lead to people feeling excluded. On our initial list of topics that we might have looked at, we also had gender, race and sexuality, issues that sadly continue to cause contention and argument in the church, at the expense of the well-being of real people.

When we say you're welcome at St Clare's, we mean it. You are welcome if you are male or female, if you are cis, trans or non-binary, if you are young, old or middle-aged, if you are gay, straight, bisexual or queer, if you feel tickety-boo, or if you're teetering on the edge of the abyss of depression, anxiety or any other mental illness, suffer with any other kind of illness or experience disability. You are welcome if you are neurotypical or neurodiverse; you are welcome if you are rich or poor, if you went to Eton or live on the streets. Whatever colour or nationality you are, whether you're an ardent believer or are just wanting somewhere to belong, you are welcome. And over the last seven years, I think we have had members who have been one or more of all those things.

Jesus tells us to stay awake. Awake, so we can be alert to injustice and oppression, to the things that exclude or imprison people, that stop them being all that God, who loves and created them, intends them to be. That for me is what it means to be 'woke', and that is what it means to be awake to Christ. I want to be alert to when racism, sexism, poverty, sexuality, mental illness, disability, neurodiversity or anything else makes people feel that they are lesser. And I especially want to be alert to when that is happening in the church, which should be the place, above all others, where all God's children are valued, loved and welcomed, just as they are.

Sadly, this commitment to inclusivity has not always made us popular. In 2019 we were so excited when the chair of the Coventry Pride committee approached us and asked if we would like to host a service for Christians attending the Pride festival. We were thrilled to be asked but said that we would first need to check with the Bishop. This we did, and after considerable thought on his part and a long conversation with me and subject to various conditions (such as no flags!), he agreed. We carefully put together a service which completely abided by the canons and doctrine of the Church of England, as well as fulfilling a few extra stipulations of the Bishop. Despite all this, when a very conservative staff member in the diocesan office heard about the upcoming service, he went to the chair of the Diocesan Evangelical Group, who wrote a letter of complaint about us to the Bishop, signed by all their members. These members included people we thought of as friends. People we had entertained in our home, people who we had prayed with, laughed and cried with. Not one of them thought to reach out and ask us about the service, or even let us know they were signing the letter. It was heartbreaking. My belief that the Church of England really could continue to be a beautiful wide-armed body, embracing a rich diversity of traditions and understandings of Scripture, began to crumble.

The irony is that, up until that moment, we had been pretty low key about our LGBTQ+ welcome. That changed. If a service that had been so carefully considered, that was so Church of England, and that had been approved by a very conservative bishop, still provoked a complaint, then we knew it was time to be more loud and proud, so that those in the LGBTQ+

community would know that we were a safe place for them in the city.

In the end, the service was wonderful, but it caused us huge anxiety. We were genuinely concerned that we might get protestors, and clergy friends came and offered to act as bouncers. No one did come and protest, and our rainbow bunting gloriously proclaimed that all were welcome. Because bunting isn't flags, right?

Adaolisa

I distinctly remember the first time I met Adaolisa. I'd been invited to preach at the Sunday service at Warwick University Chaplaincy. The chaplain was a friend of ours. She was conscious that during the long summer break, when there was no Sunday service there, several of her students were staying in Coventry, and she was hopeful that St Clare's might be a place they could come to. After the service, everyone stayed for a meal and Adaolisa came and introduced herself. She had helped with the cooking but wasn't eating, which at the time I remember thinking was a bit odd. Her name, she said, was Barbara. I was a bit surprised. Barbara was not a name I would have expected for a young black woman, but I didn't give it any more thought. We chatted, and I discovered she was in her final year, but hoped to stay on and do a Masters.

Over the long university summer, she stayed in Coventry and came to St Clare's from time to time. Even though she only came once a month or so, she was very soon a part of the community. She would regularly pop into the shop during the week, and we would chat about pretty much everything and anything. I learned a lot about the experience of being a young black woman in Britain. I also found out that she was a very talented artist, and I was soon using her beautiful artwork in some of our shop products.

One day, soon after she had finished her Masters, she started a new job, and when she was telling me about it, I realized that she was referring to herself by a different name, Adaolisa. I was a bit confused at first, but eventually just asked about it. I discovered that this beautiful Nigerian name was in fact her first name. I was then horrified when she told me that she'd stopped using it at primary school. Her teacher had found it too difficult to say, so had asked if she had a second name. She did, and so from then on she was Barbara. It was only now, as a young woman, starting her first job, that she had the courage to say, no, my name is Adaolisa.

As well as facing barriers to full inclusion in society, Adaolisa also faced barriers in church. When we ran our 'Included' sermon series, Adaolisa offered to share her story. I had assumed that she would talk about how she had felt excluded because of her name, or her ethnicity, but no, it was because of her body shape. She bravely shared her story with us. As a teenager, people at church began to comment on her weight. She became self-conscious, so tried to lose some weight. People commented more, now saying how well she looked. When she gained weight people reproved her; when she lost weight, they complimented her. The more they commented, the more conscious she became, until eventually (unsurprisingly) she developed an eating disorder. Instead of nurturing her and enabling her to flourish, the church, though well meaning, had done her serious harm. It took years for her to reach a place of acceptance of who she is, and really know her own worth, to say finally, 'I am Adaolisa. I am beloved and I am beautiful.'

Comparison is the Thief of Joy

We do not dare to classify or compare ourselves with some of those who commend themselves. But when they measure themselves by one another, and compare themselves with one another, they do not show good sense. (2 Corinthians 10.12)

Reading *Accidental Saints* was a hugely important step for me in our journey towards setting up St Clare's, and I was in awe of Nadia Bolz-Weber. Imagine my excitement when I heard she would be speaking at Greenbelt, the Christian arts festival that Naomi and I and lot of our friends attend each year. I insisted we attend everything she was part of, and the first event was a panel discussion. We arrived early to make sure we got a good spot in the stiflingly hot, overcrowded tent. Suddenly there was movement behind me as the panellists snaked their way through the crowds, heading for the stage. Nadia walked past me, just a few feet away. I was dazzled. She was tall and muscular, dressed in black and covered in tattoos. Her hair was effortlessly fierce. I hung on every word she said at every event she spoke at.

In the early days of St Clare's, subconsciously I was always comparing myself to Nadia, and inevitably I didn't fare well. There are the obvious things. I am not tall or muscular or tattooed. I doubt anyone has ever described any aspect of me as fierce. In fact, my friends sometimes refer to me as sensible Charlotte. More subtly, I was comparing what St Clare's was, and might be, to the church that Nadia founded, the House for All Sinners and Saints. Back then, we were still delighted that we sometimes had double figures on a Sunday, and the comparison began to grate.

It was Naomi (as it usually is) who brought me to my senses. She reminded me that I am not Nadia, I am Charlotte. And God doesn't want me to be Nadia, God wants me to be Charlotte. And St Clare's is St Clare's. Its own beautiful community. Inspired by other churches, yes, but not a copy of them. And no other church will or could ever be a copy of St Clare's, because its character, and the way we operate, is a reflection of its members. Members past, present and yet to join us. St Clare's works because, it turns out, I love selling things and talking to people. St Clare's works because of Naomi's extraordinary creativity and drive to get things done (left to just me, I'd still be pondering on whether starting a new church was really a good idea). St Clare's works because God sent the right people, at the right time, with all their wonderful and varied gifts, to join us. St Clare's is unique, I am unique, Naomi is unique.

A friend of ours, formerly a vicar in Coventry Diocese, has a downstairs loo with lots of framed sayings and quotes on the wall. The first time I went to her vicarage, and nipped to the loo, as I sat down, I found myself staring at these words: *Comparison is the Thief of Joy.*

These words (which I have since discovered are attributed to Theodore Roosevelt) are what I hold on to when I start to be anxious about St Clare's: when we seem too small, when we don't seem to do much, when people leave us, when things go wrong, when I look at all the amazing things my friends are doing in conventional parish ministry.

Comparison, I think, is one of the besetting sins of the Church of England, and probably other churches too. We seem unable to stop ourselves from looking at what our neighbour is up to, and worrying that we're not as good, not as innovative, not as successful. Paul, in his second letter to the Corinthians, warns us that those who measure or compare themselves to one another do not show good sense. But we can't seem to stop ourselves, not helped by the need to fill in mission statistics and, if we are stipendiary clergy, constantly having to justify the need for our very expensive presence.

Even the publication of this book has filled me with fear that people will wonder what on earth we've done that means it's worth writing a book about! Nothing we do is rocket science, and there is nothing we do that others aren't also doing in their own way and place. But that shouldn't be my concern. My concern is this ministry, this community, this vocation that God has called me to.

There is a huge amount of anxiety in the church right now. Our numbers are declining, and no one seems to know what to do about it. There's a certain structural fundamentalism, as we keep putting ever more money into schemes and plans that are much the same as they have always been, in the hope that this time it will make all the difference. We are constantly comparing ourselves to the past and to the numbers that we once had. What if we could stop comparing ourselves to what has been, and think instead about what God might want us to be in the future?

I hope that St Clare's can inspire others, as we were inspired by other churches, including the House for All Sinners and Saints, but I hope that no one tries to copy us, or compares what they are doing to us. Inspiration is good, imitation is bad, as it quickly leads to comparison, and that's a rabbit hole that is well avoided.

I am Charlotte, no one else. You are you, no one else, and praise God for that.

Acknowledgements

It's impossible to separate thanks to those who helped make this book happen from those who helped St Clare's happen, so this is thanks to everyone who has helped our vision become a reality or encouraged me to tell our story.

First and foremost, thank you to the wonderful community of people that is St Clare's, who inspire, sustain and encourage us every day. To those who showed up on day one and helped us make the dream a reality; to everyone who has joined us on the journey since; and to those who have generously allowed me to share their stories in this book.

Thank you to Morris, who always encouraged people to follow God's calling, however crazy it might seem, and who moved heaven and earth to help us make St Clare's happen. Thank you to John and Isabel, for taking a risk and graciously welcoming us to the Cathedral even though they had no earthly reason to do so. Thank you to the Bishop's Council, who discerned God's hand in our vision and gave us the money to get started.

Thank you to Auntie Jinny, whose consistent love and generosity meant we knew that we could turn to her for help when we suddenly found ourselves needing to buy a house.

Thank you to so many friends, family and colleagues who have loved and supported us on the way, and to everyone who has ever bought anything from the shop.

Thank you to Naomi's dad, much loved and missed, who, having become an author in later life, encouraged me to keep writing, even if this isn't the Dinah Doubleday sequel he wanted.

But most of all, thank you to Naomi, without whose vision, drive and many skills none of this would have been possible.